Dear Reader:

This is my true story of how I learned to have power over the abuse of my childhood. I am proud of my Bangladeshi culture, and I love my family. However, I also know that I suffered terrible abuse at the hands of those who were supposed to protect me.

I share this abuse in some detail in this book, so you can understand that if you have suffered or you know and love someone who has, there is hope for the future. Some of you may find the details triggering. Please read with care. Thank you for showing interest in my story.

— Shama Shams

What Readers Say

She Called Me Throwaway is a story of a young girl's endurance, her survival, and the crushing failures of families to confront painful secrets. But ultimately, what stays with you is Shama Shams's resilience and determination. A powerful, haunting read.

— Aamina Ahmad, Author of *The Return of Faraz Ali*

This is not only a survivor's story but a fascinating foray into Bangladeshi culture and norms. Shama paints her home country with vivid color and also with a black and white brush of sadness, as a child deeply impacted by an impoverished country and the political upheaval therein. After suffering incomprehensible abuse as a child, Shama is rescued by a father whose only intention is to bring his family to America for a better life. This book is a story like no other I've read. You will be in awe of what the human spirit can endure.

— Kandace DeLain Davis, Author of *Out of the Night that Cover Me*

How much abuse can the human spirit take without breaking? How much abuse is too much before healing becomes nearly impossible? And self-love – will that have a place in the life of a "throwaway" child as she grows into an adult? These are the questions at the heart of Shama Shams's memoir. Shams has written a singular story about surviving a childhood filled with traumas no one should have to endure, and about digging past decades of pain, shame, and self-loathing to discover beneath them the human being worthy of life and love.

— Beatriz Terrazas, Pulitzer Prize winner, *Dallas Morning News*

She Called Me Throwaway

A Memoir

Shama Shams

Editor-911 Books
Books for Readers of
All Ages

An imprint

Editor-911 Kids
Editor-911 Knowledge
Editor-911 Fiction

For Abba

Contents

1. East and West

The flames on the five candles flicker in and out as I stand there, holding my camera firmly. I don't want to miss a single minute. I want to film every inch of excitement consuming the room filled with twenty giggly girls. I zoom in on Miriam and her beautiful white dress with pastel lace trim. A matching ribbon hangs from her reddish black hair. My daughter's hair and complexion are a unique combination. She's the perfect blend of her Caucasian father and me, her Bangladeshi mother.

The party guests are dressed as Princess Bella, Snow White, Cinderella, a couple of Ariels. Disney's princesses make Miriam's party a true fairytale. Various marionette puppets hang from the ceiling inside the party room. A laced tablecloth covers the table while a princess placemat, party hat, and noisemaker are set out for each guest.

Per my instruction, Miriam's friends all smile and pose for the camera, though I know they are anxious for me to cut the Disney princess sheet cake sitting in the middle of the table. Aladdin's Jasmine is the chocolate half; the Little Mermaid's Ariel is the vanilla half of the cake. Miriam has already stuck her finger into the cake and licked the frosting several times, even though I asked her to wait.

Before the girls arrived, I spent several hours decorating the party room with streamers. Pink, blue, and purple balloons now hang on both sides of the birthday banner, a large Mylar balloon with Ariel and Prince Eric in the middle. Stacks of presents fill the corner of the room. Every so often, Miriam glances over and smiles, knowing that the gifts are all for her.

The Dallas Galleria, where we're holding Miriam's party, couldn't be further removed from the roller coaster of my childhood. I don't remember much about my fifth birthday, but I'm confident that it didn't consist of balloons, streamers, noisemakers, and my entire class.

In Dhaka, Bangladesh, where I was born and raised, the only candle that flickered in and out was the light in the lantern that lit our home. At times, the sky would light up bright, as if there were fireworks just for my birthday, but the light came from guns and bombs.

I had noisemakers at my birthday, but they were gunshots and sirens, reminding us that the war was about to resume. Usually, my three uncles, two aunts, and their children filled the house for all celebrations. But on my fifth birthday, uncertainty and fear overshadowed any celebration. There was no birthday cake. I recall that my sisters were told to be nice to me since I was the birthday girl, so they helped me dress my dolls.

Surely, on my fifth birthday, I was cautious to rip open anything in fear of what I would find, but more importantly what I would not. My gifts only unraveled a childhood filled with solitude and self-reliance. My daughters know nothing about bombs, death, poverty, or abandonment. They believe in fairy tale endings. For them and for all children, I too want to believe.

MY MOTHER, nicknamed Pinky, was the second daughter in a line of six children. My grandmother had three girls, then gave birth to three boys. I heard stories that my grandmother, Nani, gave birth to a seventh child, but she was stillborn. Amma (Bangla word for mother) was born prematurely. Over seventy years ago in Bangladesh, there were no means to take care of premature babies. So, Nani was left alone by the midwives and with no medical resources to care for her premature baby. Nani told me how she made a bed for my mother in a dresser drawer and fed her with droppers. While everyone else waited for my mother to die, Nani did not give up hope on her. I find it ironic that my Nani fought so hard for her daughter's life, but my mother did not do the same for her own children.

My grandfather gambled and was a womanizer. Nani was the foundation that kept the household together. Her decisions were never up for discussion. By the time I was born, my grandfather was bedridden with bone cancer. I am told that he loved having me on his bed, so we could play. He passed away when I was one year old.

My grandmother became a widow with six children, three of whom were still unmarried, and a huge estate to maintain in a male-dominated society. From what I witnessed and heard, my grandmother was a dominating, controlling woman. Everyone feared her, including men.

My mother in her late teen years was not interested in an arranged marriage or in following any traditional female role for women in her generation and culture. She spent her days reading the Quran and praying. She felt that any attention to physical appearance was a distraction from worshiping Allah. I never saw any pictures of my mother all dolled up like her sisters. Instead, she wore modest clothing resembling her pious life.

My mother's older sister, whom I called Boro (eldest) Khala (Bangla word for aunt), was the prettiest among the sisters. Her sharp features, dark hair, and angelic smile were adored by all. She treated everyone with kindness. Boro Khala's humility made her far superior to any other adults I knew during my childhood.

Boro Khala married a man, whom, to this day, I know as Boro Khalu (Bangla word for uncle). Boro Khalu's Bengali sounded different from the rest of us. There was a sense of presence about him. I recall his footsteps, and how all the children cleared the room if we heard his footsteps approaching us. Boro Khalu had lost his sight in one eye in some type of accident. I heard that it was replaced by a type of stone that looked like an eye. I never got up the courage to ask him to let me see his stone eye. But I did cover one of my eyes and walk around the house, wanting to experience being one-eyed. It wasn't a fun game, and soon, I forgot about his eyes.

I don't know the age difference between Boro Khala and my mother. But our culture dictated that after Boro Khala married, my mother was next in line. Marriage proposals for my mother began to come to Nani. Amma had finished her secondary school, which was equivalent to an associate degree in the U.S. Amma taught English literature at a local school in Dhaka. When she wasn't busy preparing for her class, she read the Quran and prayed. She was approaching her early twenties, which was considered old age for a woman to be unmarried. I heard from my older cousins that my mother once had a love interest. I can't even visualize my mother being interested in anyone other than herself.

Apparently, her suitor's family asked for Nani's permission, so the two could marry. However, when the groom's family requested a large dowry, my grandmother refused. My mother never spoke of this man with me. I would have liked to meet him and ask what he had found interesting about my mother. If Amma would have married this love interest instead of an arranged marriage to my father, would she have been a different kind of wife and mother? Did she still think about him and how her life would have turned out if only Nani had said yes?

My youngest aunt, Mimi Khala, was a fashionista. Her outfits were always made up of the latest fashion. Her nails and makeup—everything about her appearance —were always perfect. Red lipstick, high heels, and her hair a touch of red from henna, Mimi Khala lifted the

5

spirit with her presence. I envied her daughter. I wished that my mother was sharp and sophisticated, too.

Mimi Khala was in love with an engineer and was eager to marry. In Bengali culture, it was not acceptable for younger female siblings to marry when there was an older unmarried female sibling in the household. Mimi Khala's suitor had darker skin, and he too spoke Bangla with a funny accent. I recall watching him as he blew a puffy cloud from his mouth. The clouds smelled funny. I always knew if he was around by that funny smell. Like Mimi Khala, he was jubilant and entertaining. I didn't fear him like I did Boro Khalu. I recall that the suitor never sat still, even when he was sitting. His legs shook like he had some type of twitch. There was some anxiousness about him, as if he were in a constant search.

My grandmother became desperate to marry off my mother, so her younger sister could marry. I can only imagine the pressure and some sense of responsibility my mother felt for her sister's happiness. I wonder if my mother felt resentment, too. But like many things, my mother and I never spoke about the events leading up to her marriage to my father.

Nani was introduced to my father by a mutual friend. My father had thinning hair and a round face that spotlighted his double chin. He wore black-rimmed, thick glasses and had a gentle smile. He wasn't much into fashion or status. Abba (Bangla name for father) grew up as an orphan. Both of his parents died within a very short time of each other. I heard that Abba's elder brother looked after him, but that Abba learned at a very early age to take care of himself. I don't know how Abba managed financially, but he was an educated man. His studies took him to the University of Istanbul. He received a master's degree from the University of Chicago and from the University of North Carolina at Chapel Hill. Abba studied economics and statistics. His education landed him a high-positioned job with UNICEF as the Director of Family Planning. Abba was in Dhaka on a work assignment when his introduction to Nani took place. Nani loved my father and viewed him as her own son.

My father on his wedding day, November 1963

My father Mohammed Shamsuddin, a man who died without a country to call home, and my mother, Tajina Ahamed, married in July of 1963. They had a lovely, modest ceremony. My father wore a traditional white Sherwani, a turban, and mala (the Hindi word for garland, usually consisting of flowers bunched together on a string). My mother dressed in a gold-embroidered, red saree; gold necklaces from my grandmother and Abba, along with dangling earrings; draped in Mala with her head covered and face down; and escorted to sit next to my father. The ceremony took place on a makeshift stage where close family and elders sat to give their blessings and pray for the bride and groom.

The actual religious and legal aspects of the wedding ceremony took place earlier with a much smaller gathering of only adults, mostly male, called a Nikha. In Bangladesh, at the Nikha, the molbi recites prayers from the Quran, then the exchange of vows takes place. First, the groom is asked for his agreement to marry. The groom is asked this question three times, allowing him the opportunity to change his mind. The bride is not required to attend. She can simply send a couple of witnesses to accept on her behalf. I do not know if my mother was present at her Nikha or if Nani and Boro Khalu went in her place.

My parents didn't date. They never saw each other except for photographs until their wedding ceremony. My parents trusted Nani and other elders that they did their due diligence and matched them well.

As the elders circled around at the wedding ceremony, Abba was given a mirror, which he used to reflect on his bride sitting next to him. Then the mirror was passed to my mother to do the same. In traditional Bangladeshi weddings, the bride and the groom feed each other some sweets and exchange mala. Then they stand up and give Salam to the guests and touch the feet of elders.

I do not know if my parents loved each other. I know that it wasn't a "love" marriage, but an arranged marriage. In our culture, especially in those days, individuals did not openly display affection. Therefore, I have no memory of seeing my parents kissing or even hugging. I recall that at the age of ten, unknowingly, I told my sister that only Americans kissed. I had never witnessed any individuals with my skin color show such type of affection. The only images of kissing that I witnessed were of Westerners on TV and assumed that it was just an American thing. I remember being shocked when my sister laughed and told me that kissing was universal.

I often heard that love develops when there is compatibility, and time has passed. And that the Western concept of romantic love doesn't take compatibility into consideration. Therefore, the divorce rate of Western marriages is much higher than Eastern marriages. I always viewed my parents' relationship to be a sign of one's commitment to the entire family unit. Their interaction conveyed to me that an individual's happiness was secondary. As a good Muslim and a good daughter or son, the priority was to their loyalty to their family's name and honor.

Though I have no memory of my parents ever kissing or holding hands, I do recall that my father brought home flowers for my mother. And my mother showed affection by cooking Abba's favorite dish, beef massaman curry.

Everyone told me that I looked just like my dad. I recall years later when I was an adult and became a mom, I picked up my oldest daughter from her crib and saw

Abba's face reflected in her. It makes me smile to know that both she and I share many of my father's features.

My parents were married a month when Amma became pregnant with her first child. My eldest sister came into this world in May 1964, three years before me. My sister's given name is Aisha. I never addressed her using only her name. As a sign of respect, I call her Aisha Appa (sister). My sister's features are a nice blend of our parents, though her mannerisms resemble more our father's.

Even as a child, my sister acted like an "adult." While all the kids played in a different room, my sister sat with the adults and quietly listened. She rarely got in trouble. Even to this day, she remains our family glue, the responsible one.

A year after her birth, my mother gave birth to her second daughter, who everyone called Shati. She was a beautiful baby with fair skin and dark eyes. People said that she was the prettiest daughter of us three. Her soft, curly hair and sweet smile made everyone, especially my mother, forget that she didn't have a son.

Abba was traveling overseas for work, leaving Amma in Dhaka with the two girls. Amma had plenty of hired help, and my grandmother and aunts helped my mother by sending meals. A little over a year later, my mother was pregnant again. Prayers were said in hopes that Shamsuddin finally had a son to carry the family name.

At the same time Amma was pregnant, her younger sister was pregnant, too. My aunt wanted a daughter since a year earlier she had given birth to her son. From what I heard, Abba didn't express an interest in his child's gender. Nonetheless, Abba was again overseas on a work trip when I was born. His schedule didn't permit him to return to Dhaka for my birth.

During this time, my grandparents were separated. Nani lived in Azimpur, and my grandfather lived in Dinajpur. This was when my grandfather was diagnosed with bone cancer. His deteriorating health caused him to move in with Boro Khala who looked after him while my mother and sisters moved in with Nani.

One morning, Amma woke up from a very restless night of sleep and complaining of pain. She went into labor without a great deal of warning and a month earlier than expected. Boro Khala sent her driver to fetch the midwife, and my sisters were quickly taken to Boro Khala's house during the childbirth process.

There were no medical facilities to help deliver babies, only a group of women who learned the trade and reputation from their experience. "Bōna, ēta ciṭkāra karō nā," (Sister, don't scream so much,) the midwife said to Amma. Women being loud during childbirth were not viewed favorably, especially if you had given birth before.

My mother was always squeamish. The sight of blood made her faint. As Amma tried to not be too loud, the ladies around her prayed. They prayed that my parents would be blessed with a son. At the age of twenty-four, this was my mother's last chance of giving my father a son.

As Amma's contractions got closer, the tension and the prayer in the room became louder and louder. "Bismillah," was heard throughout the house as Amma gave her final push. I came into the world in 1967, five weeks ahead of schedule.

As I made my way out the birth canal, Amma asked, "Is it a boy?"

The midwife said in a disappointed tone, "You got yourself a throwaway baby."

The sound of disappointment filled the air. Prayers came to an end, as I cried to be heard by all, especially my mother.

After several attempts to get the operator to make the telephone connection, Nani got hold of Abba and told him that Amma gave birth.

My mother and me as an infant

The static and the hazy background noise made it difficult to hear, so Abba screamed, "Is the baby healthy?"

Nani replied, "Yes, both baby and Pinky are fine."

The call ended abruptly, and then Nani realized that she didn't tell Abba that Amma gave birth to another girl.

I heard that when they finally got hold of my Abba for the second time to tell him of my gender, he replied, "All I care is that my baby is healthy."

A month later after my birth, my aunt gave birth to a girl as well. She brought great happiness to her family, which was now complete.

Me as a baby

My birth name is Sanjukta, which is a Sanskrit name meaning "to connect." My nickname is Shama. It wasn't until my teenage years that I inquired about my last name. My sisters and I were given the last name Shams and not my father's entire last name, Shamsuddin. Amma told me that the "uddin" part of the name belongs to sons. If I had a brother, he would receive Abba's entire name. Finally, I understood why Amma treated my sisters and me as a half. To this day, I carry Abba's half last name, and my daughters carry "Shams" as part of their last name. Abba returned from America when I was almost a year old. He bought with him two sets of everything: one for me and one for my cousin. Per Amma's request, Abba brought extra plastic bottles for me. Apparently, I loved to drink bottle after bottle of milk. I was always hungry. Sometimes when we ran out of milk, Amma would fill my bottle with sugar water for me to drink. And when I finished my bottle, I threw it across the room. Amma had to keep a maid in the room with me to catch the bottle from falling on the floor and shattering. But the plastic bottles that Abba brought from America didn't help either. The bottle just landed on mosquito coils that burned near my bed. Most nights, the smell of burnt plastic and the sound of Amma yelling filled my room as I drifted off to sleep.

As a toddler, I often played with a neighborhood boy who was older than me. Apparently one afternoon, he decided to take me on a bicycle ride, and he lost control of the wheels. I flew out of the bike and landed on a rock, hitting my head. When Amma heard the commotion, she came out to check, saw my blood, and fainted. Neighbors took me to the hospital, and my head was stitched up. To this day, I have a scar on the left side of my forehead.

Perhaps my favorite memory of my childhood is going to the park with Abba and my sisters and having a race. My sisters and I raced from one side of the park to the other. I was always the last to the finish line, but it didn't matter since Abba brought the three of us ice cream as a prize for running.

My sisters and I had a cat named Pobby. She was a white cat with a fluffy tail. Everyone loved her, especially Abba. Pobby often took naps on Abba. His warm, big belly kept Pobby nice and comfy. She purred and kneaded on Abba, but he didn't mind. Pobby was the cleanest cat in all of Dhaka. Amma would give her a bath every night after my sisters and I bathed. She even powdered Pobby and made her keep the same bedtime as the three of us. Pobby didn't seem to mind the fuss, especially since she didn't have to search for food in the street with all the beggars.

One evening, Pobby was let outside to potty. When the housekeeper went outside to find her and bring her in, sirens rang. In Dhaka, it was not uncommon to have curfews to keep riots at bay. Our housekeeper ran inside without Pobby. The following morning, she found Pobby near our front door. She was injured. That day, my sisters and I screamed and cried, as my parents tried their best to mend Pobby's injuries. But she died that evening.

Abba remained in Dhaka until I was almost five years old. After he left, I wanted to relive our races at the park and jot down every detail, every laughter. Those memories reminded me of my father's unconditional love and of us laughing.

DURING MY CHILDHOOD IN BANGLADESH, some of the troubles that occurred for my family and me were because of where we lived—politics and war went together for many years. Although Bangladesh has existed as an independent country only since the late 20th century, its national character, within a broader South Asian context, dates to the ancient past. The country's history, then, is intertwined with that of India, Pakistan, and other countries of the area. The land of Bangladesh, mainly a delta formed by the Padma and the Jamuna Rivers in the northeastern portion of the Indian subcontinent, is protected by forests to the west and a myriad of watercourses in the center. In 1947, when British colonial rule ended, a downsized province of Bengal was partitioned into East Bengal and West Bengal. East Bengal was renamed East Pakistan in 1955.

In 1970, when I was about three years old, Sheikh Mujibur Rahman (Mujib), leader of the Awami League, won an electoral majority in Pakistan's general election on a platform demanding greater autonomy for East Pakistan. At the same time Zulfikar Ali Bhutto gained a majority in the West. Despite Mujib's victory, he was prevented by the Pakistan authorities from becoming prime minister of the combined state. The Awami League then issued its own plans for a new constitution for an independent state because the Pakistani army took control, and Mujib was arrested in March 1971, after a fierce crackdown.

During the early years of my childhood from 1970 to 1974, a series of disasters started in November 1970, when "the Great Bhola Cyclone of 1970," or "the 1970 cyclone" for short, struck the coastal regions of Bangladesh (then East Pakistan). It formed over the central Bay of Bengal and then intensified while traveling north toward the coasts of Bangladesh and India. It reached its peak with winds up to 115 miles per hour and made landfall on the coast of Bangladesh the following afternoon. Considered the deadliest tropical cyclone and one of the deadliest natural disasters in modern times, it resulted in widespread loss of life and property. The center of the cyclone, where the destruction reached the maximum, caused nearly 47 percent of the total population to die, and all the standing rice crops were destroyed.

As a result of the 1970 cyclone, more than 300,000 people died, and nearly four million people were directly affected with the loss of property and famine. The insufficiency of the relief efforts by the central government of Pakistan created widespread dissatisfaction among the people of East Pakistan and resulted in the resurgence of Bengali Nationalism. This is how the Awami League, the largest political party in East Pakistan, won in the national elections of 1970.

Political uncertainty and natural disasters created an atmosphere of suspicion and distrust during the early 70s. Young men disappeared from homes. Many believed that they were co-opted into the Liberation Army. In my own family, although I was too young to understand at the time, Boro Khala and Khalu feared for their eldest son's safety. In the middle of this political and social turmoil, decisions were made to secretly transport my cousin from Bangladesh to India for safety. Though I have no actual memory of this event, I am told that my cousin traveled to India by foot, rickshaw, and bus in hopes of not being detected by the Pakistani army. He remained in India without any contact with us in fear of endangering our family. Many family members assumed that he had died. However, he did return to Dhaka after the political unrest subsided.

Then in 1971, the eventual liberation war of Bangladesh resulted in the killing of millions of Bengali civilians. Bangladesh was facing serious challenges in its early independence days to tackle the increased prices of essential commodities, which were directly hurting the people.

During this time, an estimated 9.5 million refugees fled to India, as the potential for a civil war in Bangladesh grew stronger. At the beginning of December 1971, military intervention led by India on the side of the Mukti Bahini (Bengali "freedom fighters") took to the streets. Two weeks later, Pakistan forces surrendered, and the separate state of Bangladesh emerged. Sheikh

Mujib returned from captivity in Pakistan in January 1972, and became the prime minister.

But the troubles were not over. When I was seven years old, the 1974 famine was associated with the severe monsoon floods, where a significant amount of crop was damaged, which led to a further escalation of rice prices, a spike in unemployment, and reduced purchasing power. The famine caused an estimated one million deaths through starvation and diseases, such as cholera and diarrhea.

Instability in the new state was compounded by floods, famine, the assassination of Sheikh Mujib in August 1975 – shortly after he became president – and a succession of military coups with martial law and frequent states of emergency.

Like the night when Pobby was injured, curfews were the norm during the early 70s in Bangladesh. Army troops filled the streets with guns, and they marched on the empty streets. It wasn't uncommon to find tanks parked in the middle of the square. Those who ventured out after curfew did with great cautiousness and often with a note from their employer.

I don't know what happened to the homeless. And there were many people who did not have homes. The overpopulation, especially in larger cities such as Dhaka, caused limited space for housing. The UN ambassadors occupied the larger homes, and the rest of the wealthy lived in high-rise flats. This left many people desperate for their own shelter.

Nani owned the first floor of a tall building (and remained there until she was no longer able to care for herself). My parents, sisters, and I lived in a flat as well during this civil unrest. Though I don't have much memory of the inside of our flat, I recall that our balcony had several plants and red curtains.

In the early 70s, there were times when I stood on the balcony and watched the street kids panhandle and beg. Women dressed in saree with their heads covered knocked on the windows of vehicles in the street and begged the foreigners in cars for taka (Bangladesh currency). Often the police beat them as they shooed them away. The noise from the cars honking, rickshaw bells, and people going about their daily life made it difficult to hear anyone, even one's own thoughts.

Amma didn't allow me and my sisters outside much. She didn't want us to be trampled by the beggars. But more importantly, Amma felt that too much exposure to sunlight would make our skin tan. Dark skin belonged to the poor; only fair-skinned girls were considered beautiful, and it was important that my sisters and I remained fair-skinned. I envied the street kids, as they played hopscotch and roamed the streets. Amma dressed and displayed us like we were her China dolls.

As suspicion and fear of Pakistani infiltration in Dhaka grew, Dhaka police asked the public to report anyone who looked or spoke Bengal in a different accent. Abba was light-skinned and spoke Bangla with an Urdu accent. Many of our family members felt that it was in our best interest to have Abba leave Bangladesh as soon as possible.

I recall that my family moved into Nani's house again. Under military curfew, civilians remained off the streets, but not the rebels amid political uprising and looters who did not follow such rules. Vacant homes were vandalized and ransacked. And our home, after we moved in with Nani, suffered the same fate. Whenever possible, some of my male relatives went back to our flat and packed up as much of our belongings as they could.

I was four years old when we left our home and lived with various people the remainder of our time in Bangladesh. It wasn't until I was eleven when I shared a home again with only both of my parents and sisters. What took place in those seven years helped shape my ability to eventually love, trust, and overcome anything that comes my way.

AMMA WAS the shortest among her siblings. Nani viewed her as weak and often told us about Amma's birth and how Nana fought to keep her baby alive. Barely 4 feet 10 inches tall, my mother was a fair-skinned, beautiful woman. She never wore any makeup, except maybe light lipstick on a special occasion. She never cared about fashion— simplicity was Amma's fashion. Her long hair was always in a bun, and her head was always covered.

Amma had a black mole on her nose, perfectly placed as if it were a nose ring. Her large, dark brown eyes spoke without words. I could always detect my mother's mood with each dance of her pupils. Her simple glare from across the room spoke volumes. With every gesture of her body, my sisters and I knew if we were slouching or being too loud. I even knew if my dress climbed up too high over my legs by Amma's stare.

Though my mother never sought or received any mental health services, I wonder if she suffered from certain mental health disorders. I recall her random outbursts and exotic behavior.

Amma bathed me when she was hot. She came home from an outing and didn't care if I was sleeping. She dragged me out of bed, scrubbed me, and lathered me with powder.

She dressed me and my sisters as if we were her dolls. And once she was finished playing, she didn't want to be bothered by us.

People always called us dolls. The three of us girls wore matching dresses, socks, and shoes with our hair perfectly placed. Whenever company came or we visited relatives, my sisters and I were on display at Amma's feet. Amma took pride in displaying her well-mannered China dolls.

I grew up with hundreds of dolls from all over the world. Abba brought home a doll from each of his business trips before he had to escape to America. Dolls dressed in traditional garments representing Turkey, Germany, Spain, and China, to name a few. My sisters and I weren't allowed to play with these dolls, only to look at them through Amma's glass showcase.

Once a day, Amma handed our housekeeper a key, which she used to unlock the showcase. One by one, each doll was dusted and placed in its designated place. Amma always knew if one was slightly misplaced. She yelled at our housekeeper until the display was perfect.

While we lived with Nani, many of Amma's dolls were destroyed by the looters. Later, we salvaged several from our house and kept them at Nani's. Every day, Nani sat on a chair near the display case and watched her maid as she unlocked and dusted Amma's dolls.

To this day, when I see Russian stacked dolls, I am reminded of the set Abba bought home after one trip. Amma allowed me to touch the stacked wooden dolls unlike the other dolls. I loved taking them apart and lining up each doll. The father, mother, and two children —each doll nicely fit inside the other. I shook the fourth doll in search of a smaller doll, but nothing fell out. I often wondered if I was a mistake since family always seemed to come in sets of four.

As a child, I did not understand the magnitude of Bangladesh's war against Pakistan. Political uprisings have a great impact on all its citizens—young and old. Curfews prevent individuals from going to work to make wages to support their families. In desperation, often looting takes place, and store owners suffer from the loss of merchandise. The poor in the streets are left to starve, as they pray for relief from overseas.

What I knew about the uprising was only that we had to leave our home, all our belongings, and go into a hideout in order to prevent the Bengali liberation army from finding my father.

So, my family of five crammed into Nani's house. The windows were covered with old newspaper with lanterns burning low and pitch-black hallways. These are some of my memories of the war.

The wealthy hid in their homes in fear of retaliation from the freedom fighters. Streets filled with tanks, and dark houses created a sense of imminent doom across the streets of Dhaka. The sound of sirens echoed throughout the streets, letting us know to seek shelter to avoid gunfire. In fear of loud noises, I hid under Nani's bed with the first sound of the siren and remained there until the second siren rang to let us know that the fighting had paused.

In the darkness, terrified of the gunshots and tanks moving outside of our house, I laid there with my imaginary friends. I don't remember the first time I met them, but I remember that they remained by my side until I was ready to let them go. Some of them towered over me like giants. I found safety and knew that they could protect me. Some of them smiled in such a gentle way that I felt relaxed gazing into their beautiful eyes. Often, I would be too afraid to get up and go to the restroom. In fear of the darkness and gunshots, I would pee on myself knowing that Amma would punish me later. I didn't move—still in my own urine for hours at a time. Often, the fighting would last for hours, but I remained alert. I counted the gunshots and listened closely to hear if they were moving toward Nani's house.

During prayer times, the gunshots ceased, allowing people to rush to local mosques and walk out to assess the damage. Often, my mother would find me under Nani's bed during the peaceful times, soaked in my urine. Though I feared Amma's beating, I feared the darkness more. Long after the war ended, I wet my bed to avoid walking in the dark.

In the early 1970s, Abba served as the Assistant Director of Family Planning, a respected position in the government. Under duress, Abba submitted his resignation, though his resignation did not ensure his or our safety. As the rebel surge increased, homes were invaded in search of Pakistani militia hiding among the Bengalis. The military instability made it evident that my father was no longer safe and by association, neither were we. Being the youngest, I remained with my mother at Nani's while my two sisters went to live with my aunt, Boro Khala.

My father moved from one location to another to keep him safe. My sisters and I received instructions to speak to no one except our family members and to never tell anyone of our father's whereabouts. I did not understand the reason for the secrecy, but I sensed the tension and followed their directions.

During the times when I was under Nani's bed, I would see a grown-up huddle and whisper about Abba's safety. What I didn't understand at the time, but I do now, is that families with deep pockets managed to get their young sons out of Bangladesh into India or even better into the United States. Apparently, men of great influence came in and out of Nani's house. Their footsteps sounded like my uncle Boro Khalu's, so I hid from them. People's desperation to stay alive gave the corrupt political leaders and other government officials the opportunity to take bribes in exchange for docking papers for foreign visas.

One day during this unrest, my mother dressed me and my sisters in pink satin dresses and black leather shoes that Abba had bought from one of his trips overseas. My sisters and I always wore matching outfits, and strangers often asked if we were triplets. Since I was the only daughter with long hair, Amma braided my hair. She experimented with French braids and buns. She tried her best to follow pictures from magazines. She often hit me for moving and messing up her grip on my hair; I hated my long hair and wanted short hair like my sisters. However, my wide forehead; large eyes; and long, black hair completed the future Bengali bride-to-be package.

With the pink dresses on, I didn't know the specific occasion for us to dress up, and I didn't ask. Asking was a sign of disobedience, so I never asked, simply followed orders. The three of us sisters and countless relatives, packed in various vehicles with our drivers, and we headed out.

Our driver rolled down the car windows to circulate some air. The leather seats felt wet and sticky as sweat dripped down our backs. Soon, the smell of musty odors circulated, as we drove slowly down the street. The humid air brushed against my face, and I looked out the window. The streets of Dhaka did not look familiar to me. Tanks with armed men were placed throughout the street.

On this hot day, my male relative sat in the front with the driver while all the women and us children sat in the back. My khalu chatted with the guards and casually handed them a bundle of taka (Bangladesh's currency).

After a few minutes, they waved our caravan of cars through.

At the end of this long ride, we arrived at a building which looked vacant from the outside, but inside guards and countless people filled every inch of space. White aid workers from UNICEF and other charities, wearing matching garments, stood apart from the rest of the crowd.

My sisters and I stood in our matching outfits as Abba approached us. He looked helpless, conflicted, but mostly sad. In the past, I had grown strength from him, but today, he had nothing to offer me.

"I am going to America," he said. "I will send for you real soon."

"Be good for your amma and study hard."

I don't want you to go. Why do you have to go? I wanted to ask. I wanted to scream and cry, but nothing came out of my mouth. I simply gave him a hug and waved goodbye. Everyone around me cried, as Abba walked past us to board a van that drove him to the steps of an airplane. I stood there waiting and waving as the plane made it through the runway and took off. Amma stood there with us emotionless. I longed for reassurance that Abba would return soon and mostly a hug from my mother, but I knew to not rely on Amma for comfort.

After my father flew away on a plane, our caravan of cars left the airport and drove to Boro Khala's house. I recall walking into my cousin's bathroom and crying. I felt embarrassed to openly display my emotions. I feared being laughed at by my cousins. My family rarely showed any emotion, especially in public, so I wiped my tears and told myself to never forget Abba's face.

At the age of five, I knew that it wasn't safe to share my feelings, and I had to keep them secret.

GROWING UP, I did not know that there were multiple sects in Islam. My family and our ancestors were members of the Sunni sect, the largest denomination of Islam. There were a small number of Shiite in Dhaka. As a child, I watched parades of men on the streets during Muharram (the first month of the Islamic calendar and one of the four sacred months of the year when warfare is not allowed).

Geographic and historical factors had contributed to a particularly deep integration of religious structures into local communities in Bangladesh, especially in rural areas. Some historical framing is necessary for a full understanding of the evolution of Muslim religious groups in Bangladesh.

Religion has been a heavily contested element of national identity. The Bangladeshi nationalist movement was a secular one, rooted in Bengali linguistic and cultural identity, in sharp and intentional opposition to the Muslim nationalism that drove the creation of the Pakistani state.

Local religious leaders have been some of the most vocal opponents of development efforts in Bangladesh. Particularly in rural areas, local pirs and imams maligned this new vision of social progress as a foreign imposition.

Sunni and Shiite Muslims marked Muharram differently. For many Sunni Muslims, this month was the beginning of the Islamic New Year and symbolized peace and reflection. For those Muslims who followed the Shiite branch of Islam, this month represented a solemn, reflective day in Islamic history.

For Shiite, Muharram commemorated the death of the Prophet Muhammad's grandson, Hussein Ibn Ali. After questioning the legitimacy of the caliph Yazid, Hussein was murdered during the Battle of Karbala, which took place on the Day of Ashura in the year AD 680. Due to the brutality of the battle and the murder of the Prophet's grandson during a month when fighting was forbidden, many Shiites mourn and remember the bravery of the Prophet's family.

Shiite Muslims also engaged in mourning rituals. Some gathered at mosques to cry over Hussein's death and to remember the importance of what the Prophet's family did for justice, while others performed public rituals that included chest-beating, self-flagellation with chains, and forehead-cutting. When I was young, I recalled watching in horror, as men cut their chests with razor blades.

Sufism is Islamic mysticism that emphasized universal love, peace, and acceptance of various spiritual paths and a mystical union with the divine. Sufism was prevalent in Dhaka far more than I knew as a child. I recall Amma mentioning the word pir when talking about local religious leaders.

As a child, I assumed that pir was a Bengal word for guru. Recently, I learned that pirs are Sufi saints. In the late 1960s and 1970s, pirs were powerful in Dhaka, especially among the underprivileged villagers. They preached and promised salvation from the suffering. Poverty and lack of education made villagers an easy target for exploitation.

In retrospect, many of the rituals that I witnessed as a child and was forced to participate in originated from Sufism. The dancing, chanting, speaking in tongues, inhaling weed from hookah, and beating one's chest by an open fire were an abomination of the true teachings of Sufism. The self-proclaimed pirs interpreted and adjusted these rituals to solely benefit their own self-interests with complete disregard of Quranic teachings. Those who were easily persuaded were preyed upon, and that unfortunately included my own mother.

My mother was always mesmerized by individuals offering a quick fix, an easy road to salvation. Her charismatic beliefs led her to seek refuge with various religious gurus, individuals who claimed to have a path to Allah, though it contradicted Sunni's views of sainthood.

Amma often consulted a pir and sought his blessings before making any major decision. I recall taking rickshaws to Shashab, a local pir, numerous times. Our visits became more frequent after Abba left for America.

Shashab was a man in his mid-forties, but he looked much older because of his white hair and a long braid. His overweight body stayed hidden under the white, heavily starched kutas and shawl that draped over him. His meeting room displayed prayer rugs, several hookahs, and sheets that covered the bare floor. A big ceiling fan worked furiously to flow some air as people crowded into the small space.

People of various sources of financial means, including beggars off the streets, filled his room seeking his guidance. Some just sat and prayed while others stood in long lines to touch his feet. Amma touched his feet too and begged him to pray for her.

Individuals gave Shashab an offering for his prayers and guidance. Women carried their sick children; some even carried their sick parents, enduring the heat and the long journey for his prayer. They came with offerings of all sorts—a fruit, a fish, whatever valuable that they possessed in hopes of his blessings. Children with protruding bellies and runny noses, baring their naked skin, held tight to their mothers. Often, they cried from hunger, heat, and exhaustion but soldiered on with a brave face when facing Shashab.

The crowd in Shashab's room parted when Amma and I arrived and allowed us to get in the front of the line. I can only assume that the others knew of our wealth. Amma often gifted him jewels and money for his blessings.

I watched Amma fall to his feet as he touched her head and recited some prayers in Arabic. Shashab dictated Amma's emotions, her sense of being, as if she had no self-will.

Amma and I spent the entire day there as she prayed. Often, I watched the crowd slowly dwindle down, and the time slowly passed. Sitting on the hard cemented floor for hours made me tired, but Amma told me early on that any disrespect to Shashab guaranteed eternal hell.

My mother's description of hell is still very vivid in my mind. According to Amma, in hell, the body burns into ashes, and when one couldn't feel anymore, he or she lives again and burns again. The image of burning frightened me, so I forced my eyes to stay open without blinking if I could.

On our rickshaw rides back to Nani's place, Amma reminded me to not tell Nani or anyone about our visits with Shashab. I never told anyone in fear of burning in hell. But I hated Shashab for the power that he possessed over Amma.

During one of our visits to his place, Shashab advised Amma to go to his disciple named Golam in Dinajpur. Though my memory was vague, I had visited Dinajpur before with Nani and my cousins. Dinajpur is a city in northwestern Bangladesh. It lies on the Punarbhaba River, just northeast of India. It is known for its production of rice, wheat, jute, and sugarcane.

Before Amma and I left for Dinajpur, these were my faint memories of this place. After we lived there for two years, it became a place I would never forget—the place of my secrets.

2. Road Trip

I don't recall seeing my two sisters when Amma packed for what she called a short trip. She told me that I didn't need to pack my dolls because we won't be gone long. The following morning, Amma and I left Nani's house. We left my two sisters behind asleep in their bed. I learned much later that my sisters woke up looking for Amma and me to discover that we had left. Aisha was only nine and Shati, seven. They later lived with Boro Khala while I lived in Dinajpur in Golam's compound.

In Dinajpur, Islamic traditions interlocked with Hinduism. Often, traditions that one observed as Islamic were Hindu and vice versa. Most of the villagers were illiterate and depended on the religious and political leaders for assistance.

Individuals piled up; some hanging on to the side of the bus as it drove in and out of Dinajpur. With no decent public restrooms or other accommodations, few partook on such a journey in hopes of finding employment in Dhaka or other larger cities. Those who had no means of escaping extreme poverty relied on city landowners to make their annual visit to Dinajpur. Landowners paid those who supervised the harvest and collected whatever income their land produced. The rare visit of these individuals would be the only glimpse of the outside world to the residents of Dinajpur.

Nani inherited an estate called Lal Qutie, which included a mansion and agricultural land. Growing up, my mother and her siblings also visited Dinajpur, their second home away from the city life of Dhaka. My grandmother was well respected and known in Dinajpur. Her generosity was also well known. Every time Nani came to stay at her estate, the poor fled to her grounds in hopes of food, money, and medical treatment.

From the bus stop this time, with my mother, Amma rented two rickshaws, one to carry our suitcases and one for the two of us to sit. These poor, shirtless men wearing lungi, a male skirt, began paddling. We rode through small streets where people came out to look at us as we passed by because in small towns, strangers were easy to spot. Amma and I spoke Bangla with a different accent from those in the village. Kids ran around shoeless while Amma dressed me in a tailor-made dress with nice leather shoes that Abba had bought from one of his trips abroad.

My long hair nicely brushed with a big, satin bow set me apart from the rest of the village girls whose hair was in messy knots. Kids displayed stretched belly due to malnutrition while my well-fed body displayed our status in society.

Each time our rickshaw came to a stop, men, women, and even small children came up to us and begged Amma.

They kept saying, "Bōna, tumi ki kichu ṭākā ditē pārabē?" *Sister, spare us a few dollars.*

But Amma wasn't fazed by them and showed no emotion. She just shooed them away like some pesky mosquitoes and told the rickshaw driver to hurry.

Dinajpur displayed an array of greenery that could take a visitor's breath away. Long fields of grass and banana trees lined the roads, and rows after rows of bright colorful saris hung to dry. The wind blended the colors and displayed life in even the poorest parts of the village. Children waved at us, and I waved back.

Our rickshaw ride to Golam's compound felt like it took hours. At times, the rickshaw driver would stop to wipe the sweat off his brow. But he didn't miss a beat and paddled with all his might.

A crowd of children swarmed around us, as the driver slowed down in front of an old, metal gate.

Our driver yelled out, "Bhā'i, gēṭa khulē āmādēra bhitarē yētē dina" *Brother, open the gate and let us in.*

I could see some women hiding in the bushes and peeking at us. Several men stood at the front and chatted for a few minutes.

Then a small boy ran over and said, "Bābā balalēna ōdēra ḍhukatē dā'ō" *Father said to let them in.*

It took several of the men to open the gate, and our two rickshaws slowly made their way inside the compound. A couple of men came over to help Amma get off the rickshaw. Kids and women all stared at us, expressionless. Some of the little girls ran over to me and touched my satin dress and my hair. Uncomfortable feelings came over me, and I wanted to go back to Dhaka, but Amma had already ordered the driver to unload our suitcases.

Golam's compound resembled a large horseshoe or an incomplete oval. Rows of individual rooms faced the center field. The exterior of the rooms displayed chipped white paint with dried up mud. Some of the rooms looked broken down, nothing more than an unstable pile of bricks with little cement holding them from falling. Thick brush strokes of green algae covered the bottom half of all the rooms. Doors with a knob were scarce, mostly old, torn saris hung in the doorway. Chickens and other animals had the freedom to walk in and out of the rooms as did mosquitoes.

I recall that none of the rooms connected except for Golam's room which connected to another room that served as his prayer room. In the middle of the horseshoe flame danced a large fire pit. The smell of chai filled the air, as it brewed all hours of the day.

At the fire pit, women gathered and cooked meals, cleaned fish, and skinned chickens. With several clay pots and jugs of water, women cooked food to feed Golam's entire compound of followers. And at times, food was scarce, and chai and roti served on banana leaf was the meal for the day.

A few feet from the fire pit, an elevated, circular wall rose from the ground where the water well sat. Ropes with buckets tied to its handle rested on the wall when not in use. I watched women lower the bucket into the well and slowly pull it up, as water splashed out of the bucket. Carefully, they transferred the water into a different bucket either to wash clothes, cook meals, or use to bathe.

Walls made of old pieces of tin served as the bathing area. With a bucket and stick of soap, people walked inside this makeshift room to bathe in privacy. I often watched mothers give their children a bath as they screamed and cried especially in cold mornings.

Clothes hung in a long line to dry. The smell of clean clothes and array of colorful saris swung with the summer's breeze. Next to the bathing place laid a long pile of rocks for washing clothes. Women beat each piece of clothing on the rock as they scrubbed it. Twisting the garments until the last drop of water dripped out then hung on the rope. Once the bed sheets dried, women holding a corner pulled and stretched as they folded it. They worked with precision and moved flawlessly.

At Nani's flat in Dhaka, the toilet consisted of a hole in the ground with a brick on each side to elevate one's feet. We balanced ourselves while squatting over the hole to use the toilet. Afterwards, we used water to wash ourselves and wash the waste down into the hole. Only one toilet served the entire household, but it was indoors.

At Golam's compound, the toilet was at the far end of the horseshoe. A small room with walls made from scraps of tin and a broken piece of wood served as the door. Folks rested the piece of wood on the tin opening for privacy. Outside, a jug sat as an indication that the toilet was unoccupied. The jug holding water was used inside the toilet to wash one's private parts afterwards. This tin room remained pitch dark at night, so folks used a lantern.

But during the day, sunlight and air broke in through the cracks, allowing you to see the hole on the ground and below a barrel that collected human waste. Flies, mosquitoes, and all sorts of bugs and vile odor hovered there all hours of day and night.

Golam had the nicest bedroom with a large wooden bed and a long post where the mosquito net hung. White sheets and a white mosquito net gave his room a cool feeling even during the hottest of days. Next to his bed stood a fan on a small table that pointed to the bed. A dresser in the corner of the room stood covered with small dollies and various colorful bottles, and an armoire stored his clothes. The smell of incense filled the air. Next to his bed a prayer rug with a faded picture of Mecca and prayer beads rested even though his private prayer room was next door. A large window above his bed gave Golam a bird's-eye view of the entire compound.

Golam's prayer room served as a meeting place for his special guests. My mother prayed there with him on regular basis. The room consisted of prayer rugs and portable fans which often did not work due to power outage. Golam ate his meals there, and at times, Amma joined him.

Even though I was only five years old, the layout of his compound remains vivid in my mind. I once drew a picture of the compound for my therapist. And at times, I close my eyes and transport my adult-self back to Dinajpur in search of my mother but mostly in search of that little girl.

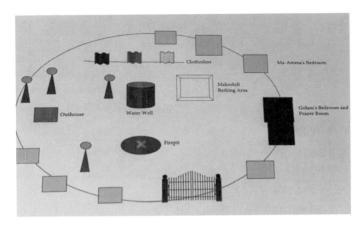

Diagram of Golam's compound

The day we arrived, the servants carried our suitcases and soon disappeared from my view. The rickshaw drivers bundled the money Amma handed them in a pouch that tied to their waist. They wiped off their sweaty faces with rags that hung over their necks. I watched the gate close behind them as Amma and I walked towards the row of rooms.

I felt exhausted from the long journey and craved a glass of cold milk. But Amma demanded that I keep up and walk with a straight back. A crowd of children and women followed behind us.

After only a few steps, I heard a steady clamp—not a joyful clamp, but a clamp that demanded attention, which I shortly learned to mean command as well. Amma stopped in full attention, and the crowd of people moved aside and created a pathway.

The sound of the clamp became louder and closer with Amma and me at the end of this pathway of people, and a man on the other end came towards us. I had never seen Golam and don't know if Amma met him for the first time on that day or not. Golam, a man in his mid-40s with white hair and a long, white beard, wearing a starched white kurta, stood with all authority in front of us. Amma immediately bent down and touched his feet, and he put his hands on Amma's head. She then stood up and signaled me to do the same. So, I bent down and touched Golam's feet and felt his hand on my head as he recited in Arabic.

Amma followed Golam without saying a word to me. Tired, homesick, and surrounded by strangers, I began to cry. I could hear a lot of chattering, but they spoke too fast and with an unfamiliar accent that I couldn't understand. The children motioned me to go with them, but I stood frozen waiting for Amma to come back, so we could go home.

I wanted my sisters and my dolls. One of the girls came up to me and asked me to play. She showed me marbles and pointed at a distance, where I could see chalk drawings on the cemented ground. Soon, another girl joined her and asked me to play, too.

They giggled and said, "Calē āsō," so I joined them.

Markings for Hopscotch could be seen on most sidewalks. Kids played with rocks for hours. But that day, our playing came to a halt when a large woman slowly made her way to us. The kids around me stood frozen like some little soldiers ready to salute.

She approached me and said, "Shama, come." Wearing a white sari with her hair in a bun and her head covered, though her sari was transparent, she called for me again. One of the girls looked at me and said, "Go, sister." I laid down my rock and walked over to this woman. Looking down at me she said, "Call me Amma."

"But that is what I call my mother," I said to her.

She grinned, nodded her head, and motioned me to follow her. I don't recall her birth name, perhaps because I only addressed her as Ma-Amma. But later I learned that she was Golam's first wife and the head wife.

On our first night, Ma-Amma showed me to my room. I recall the enormous size of the bed as the mosquito net swayed and danced in unison with the fan. My bag laid on a small footstool along with Amma's bag. I changed into my white nightgown and slippers before reluctantly making my way to the outhouse. A jug rested at the entryway of the outhouse. Within a very short time, I felt mosquito bites all over me. I ran back to my room, scratching where the smell of burning incense along with mosquito coils greeted me.

I soon dozed off to sleep. The sound of Amma whispering and talking to me woke me up. She kept saying that I was a lucky girl. "Do you know how lucky you are that he wants you?" she said.

I had no idea what she was talking about as my eyes grew heavy.

As I drifted off to sleep, I heard heavy breathing and footsteps coming towards me. I laid there still in fear and pulled the cover over my head. I heard prayers and chanting as I slowly opened my eyes under the covers and saw a shadow of a large monster approach me.

I wanted to scream for Amma, but no sound came out. I closed my eyes again, pretending to be asleep. I felt the sheet slowly being pulled off my body. From the flicking of a lantern that burnt on the dresser, I recognized the monster. For a moment, I felt a sigh of relief to know that Golam and my Amma were only on the bed with me. Amma was in a trance chanting and breathing heavily. She fell down and began to roll from side to side as her breathing got heavier. Golam said nothing as he pulled the sheet off me. My white nightgown with a lace collar felt a soft cool breeze from the fan. Golam looked at me and said to come as he dragged me to the center of the bed. He pulled up his lungi which draped over my thin legs, and he put his hand between my legs. His breathing became heavy. I tried to sit up, but Golam's weight rested on me. He pulled down my panties with one hand while he used the other hand to spread my legs. I cringed and grabbed the sheets, trying to sit up.

"Amma, Amma," I called, as I tried to search the room with the corner of my eyes. But once my panties were down, Golam used that hand to hold down my chest. I couldn't breathe and began to gasp for air when I felt something sharp between my legs. The bed shook and swayed with Golam, as the sharp pain got deeper and deeper.

My nightgown soaked from his sweat while the lower half of my body felt sticky. I didn't know if I peed or was bleeding then I felt a warm heat inside of me. Golam's breathing slowed down.

He backed off the bed and tied his lungi before walking out the door.

I couldn't move, so I laid there with my legs spread. The air from the small fan slowly dried wetness between my legs and cooled the sting. I laid there crying and calling for Amma, but I saw no one. After several hours, watching the flame from the lantern, I drifted off to sleep.

I woke up to the sound of people talking and loud noises. Ma-Amma came into the room and pulled the curtains.

With an annoying tone, she asked, "Are you going to sleep all day? This isn't Dhaka. Everyone works here."

I tried to get up, but I felt throbbing pain between my legs. Ma-Amma didn't seem to care and started taking the sheets off the bed, forcing me to get up. She then said that every morning I needed to take these off and wash them and hang them to dry.

She took one look at me and yelled out some, what I imagined, were curse words. Then she gasped and said blood stains? She ordered me to take off my nightgown, to pick up the bed linens, and to follow her. Even though I could barely move my legs, I did as she demanded.

The weather felt hot and muggy as the bright sun made my eyes water. I could see women by the fire pit, so I searched for Amma, but Ma-Amma told me to keep following. She then took me to the area where clothes are washed. I had never washed clothes before, so I stood there and watched. Ma-Amma said that next time I needed to remember what to do, as she demonstrated how to rub a bar of soap then a big flat piece of rock and beat the soapy wet cloth. With every pounding of the rock, water oozed out of the cloth. After which I needed to immerse the clothes in a bucket of water to give it a final rinse. The clothes were then hung on the rope to dry. Finally, she said that she better not see any blood stains on Golam's sheets.

As a child, I always had an abundance of imaginary friends. I recall sliding my little body under the glass coffee table at Khala's house, talking with my friends. We shared stories and many adventures together. Often, my imaginary friends looked like the images I saw on the television. We didn't have color TV back then, only black and white with very limited selections. My sisters and I weren't allowed to watch TV, but occasionally, Boro Khala would let us sit on the floor and watch. I didn't understand English, so I laughed when others laughed. I remember watching *I Love Lucy* and *The Mary Tyler Moore Show*. I loved Mary Tyler and her pretty outfits. I dreamed of being her and imagined that we were friends.

Every time Golam climbed on top of me, I closed my eyes to find my friends. I stared into their eyes, and without saying a word, they understood my pain. They took my hand and lifted me up, as if I were weightless. My friends told me to keep my eyes closed and picture the blue sky, so I did. They sang and drowned the sound of Golam's panting. At times, we ran through the meadow, chasing butterflies, and at times, we counted daisies until the pain stopped. They kept me company and remained the only constant adults in my life for many years.

In Carl Jung's book, *Memories, Dreams, Reflections*, Jung wrote, "Sometimes, I had an overwhelming urge to speak. Not about that, but only to hint that there were some curious things about me which no one knew of. I wanted to find out whether other people had undergone similar experiences. I never succeeded in discovering so much as a trace of them in others. As a result, I had the feeling that I was either outlawed or elect, accused, or blessed." I often wondered if I was the only one with such special friends. I wondered if others could see and hear them.

They kept me from noticing the blood that dripped out from between my legs. They kept me from quivering, as my flesh ripped each time Golam pounded on me, and he pulled himself deeper and deeper. They protected me. They kept me from paying attention to Golam's sweat that soaked my nightgown or how his breathing got heavier by the moment. I paid no attention to my small hands and fragile body lying lifeless waiting for it to end. Golam said nothing to me, as he didn't even notice me. Although he would say, "You whore," as he left the room.

My legs remained spread apart while the breeze from the fan cooled the sting. I didn't move, I couldn't. I just laid there, covered in my blood...wet. I never saw Amma. No one came for me. No one comforted me except for my imaginary friends.

I do recall hearing whispers in the room while he was on top of me. It sounded like prayers. And at times, I saw a shadow of a woman through the white mosquito net. I don't remember how many nights Golam came for me. I lost count, but did it matter?

One night was enough to scare me; the rest felt like ritual. Rituals kept us living and dictated our daily routine. I watched villagers wash themselves in the same way five times a day. I watched them form a straight line with the sound of Adhad, call to prayer, five times a day.

Golam never missed a Namaj (prayer) and nor did anyone who lived in his compound. Our meals, chores, even Golam's daily need to get on top of me revolved around prayer times.

It didn't take me long to learn to spread my legs for him or to learn where all the daisies were on that meadow. I learned to put a rag under me to keep the sheets from getting blood stained. I just threw away the cloth and saved myself the chore of washing the sheets every day. I learned to sleep, listening for his breath, his footsteps. I learned to cry less. Golam eventually stopped holding my neck down, as I learned that resisting him only delayed the inevitable.

I do not know why my mother did not come for me. She slept in the same bed. I do not know if she just didn't hear us or just pretended to sleep. I never called her because she taught me early on that I could not rely on her. At my birth, the midwife called me a "throwaway baby." In Dinajpur, I realized that Amma threw me away long before Golam entered my life.

Ma-Amma slept a couple of doors down from Golam's room. As a child, Amma and I sharing a bed with Golam didn't seem unusual. I don't recall giving it much thought except I do recall that others in his compound, especially other kids, were envious of me.

As if I was Golam's chosen, his favorite. I got to sleep in the master's room, in his bed, while they slept on the floor. I also sensed jealousy for my past "city" life experience. I also knew a couple of English words and dressed much nicer than all the kids in the compound. Even as a child, I knew that I held a privileged status. But

I wondered if the kids knew the level of pain that Golam caused me, would they be jealous of me still?

During mealtime, his flock of followers gathered around the fire pit. Kids sat in a straight line on the ground with banana leaves. Women walked by with a big bucket of rice and dal, and everyone received one scoop. No one dared to ask for seconds. Golam sat in his prayer room with my mother and ate chicken with rice and curry. The smell of cilantro, ginger, and cumin coming from Golam's meal filled the air, and my mouth watered.

In Dhaka, my sisters and I had made a pretend birthday cake with our plate of rice and "decorated" it with veggies and meat that we didn't want to eat. We then gave each other a "slice" of our cake. It made eating dinner fun and tolerable when we didn't care for the cooking. No one shared food at Golam's compound. Everyone gobbled up his/her serving without any complaints and with appreciation.

Before the compound, I could remember the taste of dal, chicken curry, and my favorite, phish-pash (rice and chicken) cooked with some garlic, onion, and butter. Oh, and the desserts! How I missed ice cream and mango lassi on hot days.

In Dinajpur, I had access to countless sugarcanes but no knife. It didn't take me long to learn how to peel the husk with my teeth and chew as the delicious juice filled my mouth and ran down from the side of my lips. I also learned to enjoy tea, chai. In Dhaka, only adults drank chai, but at Golam's compound, we had different rules.

I recall the feeling of hunger, not just for food, but for love and acknowledgement from my mother. Ma-Amma and I interacted regularly. She assigned chores and dictated my and the other kids' daily routines. I rarely saw my own mother except at bedtime when the two of us climbed into bed with Golam. She sat on the prayer rug or at Golam's feet most of the day. I wondered if the other women envied her for never having to perform any chores. I know that I envied her.

There were nights when the fire pit burned violently, as if the fire knew that evil was about to take place in its presence. Dancing, chanting, and the smell of wood burning would fill the air. Some of the women were completely naked as they moved, uncontrollably. Some would take hot flaming sticks and burn their bodies in the name of Allah and Golam. Utterly fearful, I stood there and bore witness to this madness. Wearing my white frock, I tried desperately to hide—to no avail. I watched my frock light up into flames, as I stood there naked like the rest. I don't recall ever burning myself; if I did, fortunately, I have managed to erase it from my memory.

Sometimes, a bag hung over the fire pit. At first, I didn't know its content. In the middle of this ritual, the bag would be lowered down, and individuals would reach inside to pull out hot razors. I, too, reached inside, burning my hands as I pulled out a razor. Perhaps the heat did not inflict as much pain; it was all painful back then, and now. Like the rest, I was forced to bang my chest with this razor and witness myself bleed. It was a symbol of self-sacrifice; it was a symbol of our powerlessness over God and Golam.

The fire would burn late into the night. At times, I would drift off to sleep as the flames bathed my skin.

Other times, I would sleep, standing up, leaning against a tree for support. Though I so desperately wanted to crawl into a bed and sleep, I knew the evil that was waiting for me in there was far greater than the fireside. Here, I was in control of my body; here, I alone inflicted pain upon myself; here, I alone held the razor that could cut through my body, my flesh. At least for that night, it was not Golam who ripped my skin and caused me to bleed. It was me.

Far away from Dinajpur, as a mother, I attended countless Girl Scout camps with my daughters, where we built fires and roasted marshmallows. I've witnessed the innocence of these girls, as they laugh and eat. I never want my daughter's perception of fire to be any different. I so desperately want to join in their fun. Instead, I find myself drifting off to my early childhood where fire only meant pain and blood.

———

AMMA SLOWLY BEGAN TO WITHDRAW. She didn't ask if I ate or had enough to eat. She distanced herself from everyone except Golam. My routine life in Dhaka, where mealtimes and bath times dictated my days, now suddenly felt unimportant. I was free to roam through the village and climb trees. My fancy leather shoes and satin dresses sat in the dresser drawer, and I, like the other kids, walked barefoot.

Sometimes, Golam came outside in the middle of dinner and said, "Which lucky kid will get to eat this?" He held up a clear plastic wrapper.

Inside this wrapper laid a yellow spongy cake with white cream filling. My mouth watered from its very sight.

Unlike the other kids, I knew its name. I had eaten it before in Dhaka. He then sat this delicious cream roll in front of us as we raised our hands hoping to be picked. He circled us, walking up and down, nodding his head with a big smile on his face. Boys and girls, all begged; we all wanted that cream puff. I remember the first time when Golam stopped in front of me as I sat on the ground.

He smiled and said, "Come."

I stood up and went to him. Holding the cream puff in one hand and me with the other hand, he led me to his room. The first time, I didn't know but soon learned to not raise my hand.

As I followed him, the other kids were giggling, and some were asking me to share. Turning my head just slightly, I smiled and waved. Golam noticed that I was distracted by the pleas of the other kids. He looked at me, and then I noticed that the gentle smile on his face was gone. He shouted, let's go with great impatience in his tone. He entered his room and almost shoved me in as he closed the door behind us. I could still hear the kids, though the wrinkling of the plastic wrapper on the cream puff brought me back into the room.

Golam asked, "Are you going to be good?"

"Yes," I replied with my hand reaching high towards the cream puff when Golam untied the string to his kurta and said get up. I climbed onto his bed. He dropped the cream puff on the ground and joined me in bed.

My face shoved against the freshly washed sheet, as he pulled my panties down. I couldn't breathe; his hand held my neck down over the pillow. The pillow and the sheet were all white and blurry. The pillow muffled my cry, as he went inside of me.

My friends whispered to me, "Daisies are the most beautiful flowers I have ever seen. They grow in the wild. They don't need anything. They blossom because of their inner beauty," and they handed me a bouquet of daises. I knew that if I kept my eyes fixed on them that soon the pain would be over. Lying on my stomach, I gasped for air and grabbed the bedpost, as Golam went inside of me.

"This doesn't hurt," I told them, or I tried to convince myself as tears ran down my face.

Once Golam's heavy breathing ended, he got up, pulled the string of his kurta, and tied a knot. I laid there against the pillow unable to move. My bottom stung, as salty tears ran down my face. Golam bent down and picked up the cream puff and tossed it to me and left.

In Dinajpur, any rainstorm caused electricity to go out and blackout throughout the village. With the lantern burning, I made my way to the outhouse late into the night.

Golam's compound consisted of over a hundred followers. I do not remember if we just had one outhouse for the entire compound or not. The outhouse sat directly across from Golam's room, making it easily accessible for me in the middle of the night.

I hated the outhouse. It reeked of foul odor which got even worse during hot summer days. I always felt sorry for the person who took the barrel of human waste and emptied it somewhere. I do not know where. Like most societies, human waste is considered the dirtiest of all. The individual who had the unfortunate job emptying the barrel was considered subhuman.

The outhouse was an enclosed area with only a hole in the ground with two bricks on each side to help one elevate and scout to release herself. There was a barrel placed below the hole that collected the waste. A tiny pathway led to the barrel for one to replace full barrel with an empty one.

There were times when I was using the toilet, I would hear a woman underneath yelling that she needed to replace the barrel and to hurry up. I could only hear her and never tried to look for her.

At times, when Golam would position me in a way that was utterly painful, I fought him furiously. Even my friends couldn't distract me or make it easy for me. They would give up and sit there helpless and watch me endure Golam's beating.

I would tell them that it was all right. "You can't protect me all of the time."

Golam would get up and spit on me. He reminded me how fortunate I was that he even wanted me. "You are lucky... you are nothing more than a whore...you bitch," he uttered in Bengali.

I could hear his violent outburst even though my friends held my ears shut tight. At sunrise, Golam told Ma-Amma that I did not cooperate.

As a punishment, with a rope tied to my feet, I walked down a long, dark passageway inside a tunnel. There, a woman led me down this pathway. At the end of the pathway stood a barrel which collected human waste since it sat underneath the pit.

The vile odor made me vomit uncontrollably. The woman leading me there pulled a rag over her mouth and nose as she untied my feet. She took that same rope to tie my arms around the barrel.

I stood there facing the barrel with my arms stretched wide. My face touched the barrel and the ghastly smell that penetrated from its content. I stood there gasping and gagging for air. I stood there for hours on end.

After some time passed, the woman showed up with her mask on and untied the rope and led me back. One of the women from the compound hosed me down, though the smell of foul human waste consumed me. After bathing me, she put sugandhi, scented oil that Golam preferred, on me. That evening, I positioned myself whatever way Golam desired.

I looked to my friends for love and escape; I looked to myself for protection, and I surrendered to Golam for food. At the age of six, I learned to survive. It wasn't until much later in life that I learned to live.

THOUGH NANI LIVED IN DHAKA, she made sure that Lal Qutie, another home of her family's in Dinajpur, had a caretaker. She fought many legal battles against my grandfather's family to keep the estate in our family. To ensure occupancy, she had a live-in caretaker who looked after all the workers on the field and made certain that no one stole or shortchanged her crops.

Right before Nani's annual visits, her estate would receive a major overhaul. Folks prepared for days before her arrival in fear of getting fired. Nani had a gentle side, but also a very firm side which didn't allow for too much disorder.

Nani didn't follow the traditional Islamic women's role. She maintained all the financial exchanges, oversaw her children's education as well as their arranged marriages. She was a stubborn and strong-willed woman.

Nani, this tiny lady with a fair complexion, white sari, and no makeup, stood with authority. My grandfather, Nani's husband, fell sick early on, and Nani slowly took over managing the household finance. Later, I heard that my grandfather's gambling and unnecessary spending forced Nani, out of necessity, to take over household finances. She didn't want our family wealth to be in jeopardy; therefore, she started to take control of finance long before he got sick.

I have no memory of my grandfather. His cancer advanced quickly. A few months before my birth, he became bedrest. I heard that I sat on his bed, and he played with me. He died before my first birthday.

Everyone feared Nani, including my mother. Nani didn't like that my mother left my two sisters and moved to Dinajpur to live with Golam, but for reasons I do not know, she didn't insist that we move back either. I looked forward to her visits to Dinajpur. It gave me the opportunity to hear about my sisters and leave Golam's compound to stay at Nani's estate.

Unlike Golam's compound, Nani's house had an abundance of food, and her maids attained to my every need. I recall telling Nani that Amma said eggplants were too expensive, but I really wanted some eggplant. That evening at Nani's, I had eggplants cooked for me in a variety of ways. Nani's cooks made eggplant curry, baingan bharta, and fried baingan— and it felt like heaven.

Occasionally, Amma let me spend the night at Nani's house. I remember telling Nani that I wanted to be in school like my sisters. Apparently, Boro Khala had enrolled my sisters at a Canadian school named Maple Leaf International School. Founded in 1972, Maple Leaf was one of the most prestigious English medium schools in Bangladesh. It followed the British curriculum. My sisters were learning to read and write both English and French. I didn't even know the Bangla or English alphabet.

Nani's stories of family sufficed me until her next visit. Nani told me that my youngest aunt and her family, my cousins Rafat and Amna, moved to Abu Dhabi for my uncle's work. Listening to Nani, I couldn't help but envy my cousin's life. She wore fancy clothes, attended fancy schools, and could speak English. Not to mention, she overshadowed me physically in every way possible. Her long legs, long hair, her ability to speak English, and tell funny jokes, my cousin naturally received the spotlight. Nani often bought my cousin's hand-me-down clothes and shoes for me, though they were too fancy to wear in

Dinajpur. Though I envied my cousin for various reasons, it was mostly because she lived with both her parents and traveled on airplanes to various foreign countries. I missed Abba and had forgotten how he looked.

My sisters sent letters with Nani for me, but I could not read them. At six, I had no schooling and couldn't identify a single letter of the alphabet. I don't recall if there were any schools in Dinajpur. Survival took precedence over any schooling in Dinajpur. Perhaps ignorance kept us from knowing what we could not even dream of attaining.

Nani also bought some nice tailor-made outfits that she had made for me. My appearance appalled her. "She looks like one of the village girls. She looks like a servant," Nani told Amma, referring to me.

Nani said nothing about how thin I looked from not eating, only that my unbrushed hair and dirty dress disgraced our family.

One evening after dinner, Nani and I sat while she drank tea and I ate biscuits, just talking. She told me about my sisters and cousins in Dhaka. I remember telling her that both Amma and I slept in Golam's room. He had the "best room" I told her. Nani looked uncomfortable but said nothing. I continued, "Sometimes Golam sleeps next to Amma, and sometimes he sleeps next to me."

"Don't talk about those things," Nani said with utter disgust in her voice.

I felt ashamed that perhaps I said something that I shouldn't have. Nani reached for her prayer beads and started to slowly stoke one bead as her finger slid to the next and her lips murmured some prayers. She gazed out the window, as if we were no longer in the same room. I felt as if Nani too left me for a moment which felt like eternity.

After she finished her entire circle of beads, she turned her head back from the window and asked, "Have you said this to anyone?"

In fear, I simply shook my head left to right without saying a word. Who would I say anything to? I wanted to ask. Everyone at Golam's compound knew that Amma and I slept with Golam.

"Jaghan'y! Āllāha tādēra gunāha māpha karuna," she said. It is a gesture often used in disgust, and it is a phrase that asks for Allah's forgiveness.

Nani followed with her command with her back stretched and her entire five-foot body grown into a giant. She told me, "Never talk about this to anyone."

That entire evening, I laid in bed and watched Nani pace back and forth with her prayer beads in her hand, and her lips moved, as she recited prayers all night. At times, Nani came over to me and blew air on my face. Nani bestowed her prayers on me; then she turned her head, first left then right, and blew prayers on the entire room. I didn't know what she was saying, but it always made me feel safe. Nani had the power to dictate her wishes to her sons, daughters, housekeepers, to so many that I knew that she had the authority to blow devils and sins away from me as well.

The following morning, I quietly ate my paratha and eggs. I savored each bite before heading back to Golam's place. But I was worried that I upset Nani, and I might get in trouble. I didn't want her to tell Amma what I said about Golam.

In fear of making Nani mad, that was the last time that I spoke to anyone about my sleeping arrangements at Golam's compound. And Nani didn't mention our conversation either until many years later.

I hated to see Nani go. While she was in town, I had an abundance of food to eat and housekeepers who washed my sheets and made my bed. But mostly, I loved her and her straightforward, confident attitude. I always cried when she left. My only friend, Raja, and I would run after her car until it disappeared, leaving us with only a cloud of dust. I cried some more knowing that I had no other place to call home except with Golam and Amma. And I had no bed except with Golam and Amma.

Nani often took young children from Dinajpur back to Dhaka to live with her. Parents gladly handed over their teenage boy or girl to her in hopes of getting an education and the opportunity to live in the city. Nani paid for their education, and a young boy or girl worked by running errands and doing chores at Nani's house in Dhaka. Nani always had a handful of kids working for her. Many remained very devoted to her long after they became an adult. On several occasions, Nani even arranged marriages for several of her help. She purchased new saris and some gold for the bride and made the marriage arrangements. She also didn't hold back if she felt they needed good disciplining. Often, I heard her scolding them as if they were children. I guessed they knew that at the end of the day, Nani's heart and intentions were well-meaning.

I begged her to take me back with her and told her that I would work like the other kids.

"I can give you massages," I pleaded.

I just wanted to go to school and see my sisters. But Nani always said no. Perhaps Nani feared that if Amma remained in Dinajpur without any of her children, people in Dhaka would gossip and eventually words of Amma's infidelity would reach Abba. I don't know her real reasons since we never discussed it. As I think back, we didn't talk much about anything significant. Those who knew pretended to not know, and those who didn't know remained blissfully ignorant.

As days went by, I feared that I had forgotten how Abba and my sisters looked. I could no longer remember them and feared that they too had forgotten me. It had been almost three years since I left Dhaka. I no longer looked like the girl that arrived in the rickshaw that hot summer day. Something changed inside of me that I still cannot explain. I felt alienated from the kids at Golam's compound because I was never one of them. I was an outsider from Dhaka. Except for Raja, no one wanted to play with me.

Raja was a fatherless child, perhaps motherless, too. He was nine years old, but he was a man. His tiny, thin build with short hair, which was always covered in dirt, could easily go unnoticed by his big smile and large, brown eyes. He, like the rest of us, was a faceless, parentless child who had no last name and nothing in his possession, including his body. He and I became friends soon after Amma and I moved to Dinajpur. We had only one secret between us. I never told him about my imaginary friends.

Raja ran all sorts of errands for everyone. Need something from the market? Send Raja. Need someone to go fishing? Send Raja. Need someone to sweep, mop, paint? Raja. I don't know if he was ever allowed to be a child. But I do know that he loved to laugh. The other kids whispered and talked behind my back. They were afraid that I would tattletale on them to Golam if they didn't follow his orders. I desperately wanted to make friends. I didn't know how to play all by myself. I had always had my sisters and my cousins, but nothing was the same in Dinajpur.

I also knew that I no longer belonged in Dhaka. I was no longer a well-dressed, well-mannered, little girl who always crossed her legs when sitting. I no longer wore leather shoes. I didn't have any that still fit my callus-filled, dirty feet. The few English words that I knew, I had forgotten. Amma had shaved my head countless times due to head lice. The small glimpse that I got of myself in a mirror made me miss my pink satin dress and matching ribbon that draped over my neck.

The kids in Golam's compound didn't go to school. We all had chores to accomplish every day which included washing clothes, doing dishes, and prepping veggies and sometimes meat for cooking. We had countless tasks. I recall collecting wood and filling barrels after barrels with water from the well. At times, we went fishing and brought back a large load. But the kids didn't receive any meat during mealtime. The fish we caught provided Golam and his special guests a delicious meal.

There were times when the village kids let me play Hopscotch with them. I wasn't very good at balancing and would tumble over, as I tried to hop from one box to the next. The other kids would burst out in laughter. With a skinned knee, I would try again. And there were times when we climbed coconut trees. We plucked coconuts from the tree and banged them with rocks or whatever we could find, hoping to crack them open. At times, we used our teeth to pry open a small hole that allowed the coconut water to escape. We scraped the juicy coconut with our teeth and ate it slowly to enjoy each bite.

Sometimes if we got too distracted with our playing and didn't report back to Ma-Amma, she didn't hesitate to demonstrate her authority over us, nor did the other men. The husk from the sugar canes made switches for beating.

On countless occasions, those switches ripped my skin. The sharp edges of the switch left my skin with cuts, like paper cuts, except these cuts lined up like lines on a page and my body ripped with every line. Soon red, bumpy, bloodstained lines covered our bodies.

I always hid my face when a beating started; I feared the switches hitting my eyes and blinding me. As a girl, I was of no use. I could not imagine a life as a blind girl.

The reason for our punishments varied. For me, it could be that I didn't properly satisfy Golam's sexual desires. It could be that I resisted him too much, and he complained to his wife about me. It could be that I bled too much and got Golam "dirty" during intercourse. He nor Ma-Amma needed any justification for their actions, and I did not ask for one.

The words "Āmākē kṣamā kara" (forgive me) echoed throughout the village, as I watched women lined up in rows. They lined up not to pray but to be beaten to a point of unconsciousness. Their dark-skinned bodies softened the deep red blood that dripped from their skin. For me, the red blood served as a great contrast on my fair skin.

I learned early on to play dead. We remained still on the ground. Some of the kids begged and said, "Āmākē kṣamā kara" in hopes of mercy. No one had mercy on us, not even God.

I had different chores from the rest of the kids. As Golam's "chosen one," my responsibility consisted of cleaning after him, cleaning him, feeding him...the list went on. Golam's wife taught me how to serve him. If she wasn't pleased or if he showed dissatisfaction, it warranted punishment.

Golam also had strict rules for all of us at the compound. Some of his rules prohibited us from leaving the compound unaccompanied or sharing our food with anyone, especially since starvation served as a form of punishment. I never followed the "rules." I shared my food with the starved kids all the time. Raj and I hid food in our clothes and gave it to others.

Showing disrespect to Golam resulted in more punishment. If I cried too much or resisted his sexual advances too much, he slapped and kicked me. After which, someone escorted me to solitary confinement.

After being beaten, the sting came as buckets of water mixed with salt were poured on us. The salty water stung my body and caused my eyes to burn. I cried and called for Abba, my imaginary friends, but never my mother. I cried but never uttered the words, "Āmākē kṣamā kara."

One punishment was hard to forget. Tiny light escaped through the cracks above me as the water flickered below. I hung upside down inside a water well for hours at a time. My feet strapped to a rope and hung from a pole above. I do not remember how long I hung there or how many times I found myself in the well. But I recall that it became a familiar place for me. I felt protected by the walls of the well, like some shield protecting me from head to toe. My arms dangled as it swayed around. My body so drenched with sweat that often the rope felt loose around my wrist. I didn't know the depth of the water below me. And I didn't care. I imagined jumping into the narrow pool and splashing in the cold water.

My frock draped over my face with my panties exposed. At times, I couldn't help but pee, and my warm urine ran down my body, as I tried desperately to not let any make it to my mouth. And I knew that peeing resulted in more beating for contaminating the well water.

I never minded being alone. I always had my imaginary friends to keep me company. At times, I stayed in a small, underground hole. I drew there, using a stick, or I used my fingers and drew pictures in the dirt. In the hole, we played for hours, as my friends told me stories

63

and made me laugh. Unfortunately, my solitary ended at sunset. After bath and putting on my nightgown, with no food or water, I found myself on my back once again for Golam.

As days went by, I no longer wore leather shoes or tailor-made dresses. I no longer looked like a girl from upper class; I too became another nameless, faceless village girl.

———————

SOMETIMES UNICEF WORKERS visited our village. They dressed in uniform-like clothes which made it easy to spot them. The word of their arrival traveled fast. The other kids and I swarmed the aid workers and begged. We didn't ask for anything specific; we only knew to say please in English. It didn't matter what they gave us, but an item from America had value. Sometimes the aid workers gave us candy. I savored the candy and held it in my mouth if possible, hoping to keep it from melting. I loved the colorful wrapping paper that covered the candy. Secretly, I had a small treasure hole in the ground, where I kept candy wrappers, and visited it often. I took a big breath and closed my eyes and imagined living in America.

One day, Raja came running, looking for me. I was near the water well helping the women wash clothes.

"Shama," I heard his squeaky voice from a distance.

He was too afraid to approach me in fear of getting in trouble for disturbing me while I worked. Raja wore a gray tank top and lungi tightly fastened for swift movement. His stretched belly, dark tanned skin, and skinny build hidden in the bushes made it easy for me to spot.

That day, the women at the water well were too busy chatting among themselves to notice me or hear Raja.

"I forgot something," I said, careful to not say it too loudly, so they couldn't hear, but not too quietly, so they knew that I said something as I got up and ran to Raja.

"Lots of foreigners are here," he told me with an excited voice as he ran and I followed, wearing a yellow frock with my long hair pulled back in a ponytail and barefoot.

We ran down through the crowded streets to find a huge gathering of people. Raja and I jumped to see over the crowd as we pushed our way through. We could see men and women wearing shirts with large letters on the back. Rows of tables and Bengali men walked around with clipboards. The guards with sticks yelled at the crowd, and people pushed to form a line. Women with crying babies came out of the makeshift clinic. The Bengali man yelled at me and Raja to go away, or he would give us a beating. Raja and I didn't care. We stood there eagerly for what I didn't know. I loved staring at the men and women's beautiful golden hair and white skin. Some of them tried to say a Bangla word or two, and we all giggled at their failed attempt.

A foreigner saw me and Raja and waved us over. Raja hesitated, but I had seen foreigners before in Dhaka.

"Āsā," I said to Raja and ran up to the table when, with broken Bangla, this man reached over to me and asked, "Āpani kēmana āchēna?" (How are you?)

"Bhalo," I replied.

He opened a box, reached inside, and pulled out a small box of crayons and a coloring book. Raja ran up to the table and stood next to me as soon as he saw me getting a present. The foreigner smiled and gave Raja the same.

Overwhelmed with excitement, Raja and I ran to a secluded place to look at our gift. The box had red, yellow, blue, green, orange, brown, black, and purple crayons inside. I pulled each one out of the box one at a time and slowly smelled them. The fresh, crisp smell was like nothing I had ever smelled before. The coloring book had pictures of little girls wearing beautiful dresses with bows on their hair. Some of the pages had grownups, too.

As Raja and I carefully flipped the pages, we heard voices at a distance.

In panic, Raja said, "We have to hide these."

With our fingers and sticks, we dug a hole in the ground and buried our treasures. He and I visited our hidden treasures often, but neither of us used any of the crayons or wrinkled the pages in our coloring books. We knew that if Golam got wind that the aid workers gave us a gift, he would make us all surrender them to him. So, Raja and I promised to keep our treasures a secret.

At times, Abba sent with people traveling to Dhaka money, birthday cards, and boxes of chocolate from America. Nana forwarded Abba's gifts to Amma and me. Amma willingly gave Golam everything, including my birthday cards. Golam always kept the candies for himself and his guests to enjoy. I recall watching him sit in his prayer room with my box of chocolate candy. Abba also sent birthday money to me. I never got to keep the hundred takas that Abba sent, nor did I get to taste the candy. Sometimes, after he inspected my birthday card, even though he could not read English, Golam would let me have it. I would proudly walk around with my card and show it to everyone.

Abba's cards

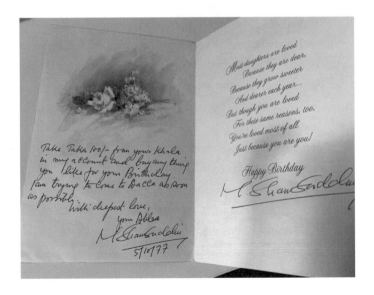

Afterwards, I hid it along with the coloring books and crayons. I still have those birthday cards from Abba, and now I can read his messages to me.

All the kids in the village were jealous of my pretty card from America. But Golam would say, "He is never coming back to get you," referring to my father. "I am sure that he already has some pretty American girl for his daughter."

I OFTEN WONDERED if Nani took pity on me every time she came to Dinajpur; I begged and pleaded with her to take me back to Dhaka. I knew that Amma wouldn't miss me. She barely noticed me. Dhaka meant seeing my sisters, attending school, wearing fancy clothes, eating whenever I was hungry. Dhaka meant everything that I didn't have and certainly wouldn't dare to ask of my mother. If pity meant not feeling left out, I didn't mind.

I don't recall why during one particular visit, Nani was persuaded to take me since she had refused many times before. But she agreed that I could live with her at her flat in Azimpur.

Nani approached Amma and said, "Shama needs schooling. She can live with me."

Amma seemed indifferent. I am sure that she felt a sense of relief to not have me around. But Amma rarely did anything without consulting Golam, so she told Nani that she needed to ask Golam first.

I tried to wait patiently, but the butterflies in my stomach gained force with each passing minute. "Thank you, Nani," I said countless times. The possibility of leaving Dinajpur, the possibility of never having to share a bed with Golam potentially could be the best gift anyone had ever given me.

Nani knew of my desperation, and as I think back, her offer to have me live with her relieved her of some of the guilt and shame that she felt towards her own daughter's sordid affair with Golam. She even offered to give Amma and Golam some money in exchange for me.

When Amma told me that Golam agreed to let me go, I cried. I don't recall if I felt happiness or sadness, but I remember sobbing. I couldn't wait to tell Raja and the other kids at the compound. Though they shared in my excitement, I felt their envy like the envy I felt towards my sisters and cousins.

That very evening, I filled my suitcase with a couple of worn-out dresses and those birthday cards that Abba had sent to me over the years. Afterwards, I walked around the compound, the well, the outhouse, the choked lines that we drew on the pavement to play Hopscotch; I looked around as my mind photographed it all for safekeeping.

I don't recall if I was sad or relieved to be leaving Dinajpur. I wanted Amma to come with us, but her devotion to Golam outranked her daughters. So Amma simply gave me a hug and a cream puff, the type that Golam used to lure us to his bed. But this time, I didn't have to perform for him; it was mine.

Amma said, "Golam got this for you."

Golam wasn't there to say goodbye to me. But I could see him in the distance. His white starched Kurta was easy to spot. In an unceremonious way, I got in Nani's car after almost three years. I was finally headed back to Dhaka to be with my sisters. As the car pulled away, Amma waved, and Raja and the other kids followed us until they got lost under a cloud of dust.

A few miles into our drive, the wind picked up, and the sky grew dark.

The driver told Nani, "Bṛṣṭi jhaṛa āsachē." (Rain is coming).

He advised Nani that it would not be safe for us to drive in the rain. Nani instructed the driver to hurry up. But in a small village, like Dinajpur, the street beggars, cows, and rickshaw made weaving through the crowd a long process. The sky began to darken, and my stomach sank. The trees swayed in unison as debris rose from the ground and swarmed around our car.

The driver asked again, "Ma, should I keep going?"

After a moment of silence, Nani replied, "Turn around."

As we headed back to Dinajpur, my stomach sank even further if that was possible. The driver pulled up to Golam's compound and honked his horns. A couple of men opened the gate as strong wind and rain fell.

Nani looked at me and said, "We will try tomorrow." Then she and the driver pulled away, leaving me alone to face Golam and my mother.

The wind was picking up fast. The clothes from the cloth line were flying everywhere. Kids and women were trying to collect things before they blew away, but dust filled the air, making it difficult to see. I hurried down the pathway with my suitcase.

The lights in the lantern flickered and shortly after darkness consumed the halls. The fire pit blew smoke, and the entire place resembled that of an abandoned lot.

The wind pushed against me and made it hard for me to stand straight. I wobbled as I tried to hold on to the walls. I felt the doorknob and entered. It was Golam's room. My mother wasn't there, only Golam in bed. He sat up as I walked in.

He leaned his head back and with a grin said, "You came back to me. You can never escape me."

That was my final night in Golam's bed and the final time that he forced himself on me. I looked for my friends that night to only apologize for not taking them away like I promised. I apologized for being weak.

The following morning, mud and dirt filled every walkway. Broken trees and makeshift houses covered the ground. Animals and humans all walked around confused and ready to survey the damages. The damages were enormous, but rebuilding was norm for these people. They were used to starting over after every rainstorm, especially during monsoon season.

I wasn't certain if Nani and her driver could make the drive to Dhaka. I didn't know if the road would be clear or filled with debris. I anxiously waited with my packed suitcase. Amma wasn't very happy to see me back. All the other kids seemed angry with me for leaving, then returning. I was already marked as an outcast, no longer a part of Golam's group of followers. Except I was never Golam's follower, I was there because of Amma.

Mid-afternoon, Nani and her driver showed up. He again put my suitcase in the trunk as I said goodbye to

Amma. With a bag filled with some puri and some dates, I got in the car. Kids again followed our car as it pulled away. I could see Raja in the far distance waving his hands. I felt bad leaving him behind. He and the others chased our car for a while, and eventually, they were lost with the dust.

I turned my head away from the back of the car and looked ahead to the new road that was before me. I had no idea what my future would entail. I didn't know how my life would be at Nani's place. But I did know that I was no longer near Golam, and I was much closer to my sisters. And I was getting a little closer to Abba and to America.

Our drive took hours with many stops to clear out the street before our car could pass through. Nani gave street beggars money to help our driver clear the streets. There were many individuals willing to help in hopes of a few takas.

With windows rolled down, the hot air filled the car. Bugs flew in and out, and I tried to fan them away. At every stop, children and women barely dressed and men with one leg banged on our door and reached their arms inside our car in hopes of food or money. Kids yelled "gari" (car) out loud, and people emerged from all around. Seeing an automobile was still a novelty in those parts of the village.

Nani's car wasn't fancy. I don't recall the make, but it was a white sedan. No one ever sat at the front with the driver. It was not appropriate for one to sit next to someone you have employed to cook, clean, garden, drive, and so on. Furthermore, it was not appropriate for a woman to sit next to a man. So, Nani and I sat in the back while the driver drove. From the back seat, Nani continuously told him to slow down, turn here, go there, and he followed her commands without any hesitation.

I ate my puri and patiently waited to arrive in Azimpur. I didn't recognize the streets. The crowds of people grew, as we got closer to the city. The streets were filled with rickshaws, scooters, bikes, cow carts, buses with people hanging from all around, and masses of people. Our car made it through the street slowly, inching its way a step at a time.

Finally, I was on the road to becoming a city girl.

3. Mama

Nani's flat was located near major streets and shops with vendors frying samosa and luchee; some sold fresh coconut and hot tea. I could see men walking around wearing lungi and flip-flops, some shirtless due to the heat; women balanced water buckets on their heads and walked through the crowd with great ease while others sold random plastic containers and books that they probably got off the black market to sell. Colorful saris hung at the distance, and each person walking by was stopped and asked to come in to shop.

Other vendors rolled their carts and yelled out that they had fresh veggies and fruits for sale. And rows after rows of rickshaws stood in a line, waiting for a customer. The sounds of horns and whistles were never-ending. Even with our home or car windows shut, we could not escape the hustle of the loud, congested streets of Dhaka. Only five times a day did silence fill the air, as the call to prayer echoed throughout the city, telling people to pause. It was that moment we were reminded that Allah was ever so present and a part of our daily lives.

While most chose countryside homes away from the crowds, Nani preferred the crowded city life. It gave her the freedom to commute without long waits. That first day, memories of Nani's flat came back to me, as the driver pulled up to the gate. The big, heavy, green iron doors and windows with rod iron panels and the building were surrounded by an open sewer line where water and waste constantly flowed.

Nani looked at me and said, "Wait in the car."

She walked in and her housekeepers came out to get our suitcases. Nani came back out and motioned me to come inside.

I walked in through the back of the flat which was the kitchen and main quarters. A large sink covered half the wall to my left where metal shelving stood, filled with jars and spices and a big clay stove in the center with several stools surrounding it. Clean dishes and glasses rested on a small table along with a bowl and a jug. The kitchen led to my eldest uncle and his wife's room. It was a large room with a canopy bed. Two large windows on each side of the room allowed the sun and fresh air into the room. The windows had metal bars. The room had a glass showcase which consisted of mostly dolls that Abba had bought back from his various trips overseas. When Abba fled to America and we had to abandon our home, Nani took the showcase and had been taking care of the dolls for us.

There was a large dresser in the room. On top sat some bottles of perfume and nail polish. My mami (aunt) loved to dress up. Every day, she dressed up in her fancy saris and wore makeup. She loved to go shopping even if she didn't buy anything; she loved to go to the nearby market. New Market was a large bazaar filled with various vendors selling saris, imitation jewelry, and shoes. Mami knew them all and bargained with the vendors for discounts. Sometimes, I would join her on her shopping adventures. The vendors somehow knew that she had money to spend. They leaped out of their shops and chased her down, telling her all the new items that arrived.

The crowds at the New Market intimidated me. With a blink of an eye, one could easily lose each other, so I hung on to Mami's sari, as if it was my leash.

From their room was even a larger room that belonged to Nani. There stood a large canopy bed that sat very high from the ground where Nani slept. I recall that I needed to use a step stool to reach her bed. Nani had a small bed put on the other side of her bed for me. It was low to the ground. A tiny pillow and several blankets sat on top. A large window, which I stared out of every day, was directly across from my bed. Both of our beds faced the only television in the entire house. TV aired only in the evenings, every day except for Friday, Islamic holy day; and sometimes on special occasions, we would have some TV on Sunday. When the TV aired, the entire house would come to a standstill. Even the housekeepers filed in to get a peek, and if Nani were in a generous mood, she would allow them to sit on the floor and watch. All American shows were censored. Reruns of Roger Moore's *The Saint* were edited and aired for only thirty minutes. Any murder scene or scenes of criminals escaping were censored in fear that they would give thieves ideas. And all romantic scenes were censored due to strict Islamic tradition.

Next to the TV stood Nani's armoire, a full-size metal locker where Nani kept all her valuables, such as gold bars. Her perfume bottles were all new and still in their original packaging. Nani saved them as treasures. She wore the key in a chain and hid it inside her bosom. Her gold jewelry, expensive perfume from America, important documents, and cash were inside, and no one was allowed to open it. Nani's room led to my two younger uncles' rooms. Nani's middle son was single and was in law school, and her youngest son was still in upper level, equivalent to high school. Their room had a door that led to the back of the flat where rows of vendors were open for business all hours of the day and night.

As I walked into the house through the kitchen, Nani's bedroom door slammed. I stood awkwardly not knowing where to go. I could hear loud voices from behind the door.

One of my uncles in a screaming voice asked, "Why did you bring her?"

Nani replied, "You don't have to worry. She will stay with me in my room. No one must worry about her. I'll take care of her."

"Great, now Pinky Bo (what he called my mother) has none of her kids to look after. She has no responsibilities."

I stood there in the hallway listening to them with my stomach sinking. I wanted to scream out to them and say that I would be good. *Please don't send me back to Golam.* But I said nothing.

The first several days at Nani's, no one spoke. My uncles ate quietly and left the table without saying a word. Nani said nothing, too. The quietness made me anxious and worried about Nani having a change of heart.

Nani's housekeepers looked in on me as one of their own. I hung with them most of the time. There were no small children in Nani's house. My eldest uncle's wife was pregnant so took a lot of naps. In the afternoon, the house would be dead quiet with everyone napping. I pulled out my paper dolls that Abba sent and played alone. Several days after my arrival, Nani told me that my sisters were coming over for dinner.

I hadn't seen my sisters for almost three years. While I climbed trees and hung out with the village kids, my sisters attended school and learned both English and French. I didn't know if we could recognize each other. I didn't own any pretty outfits; most were ruined in Dinajpur, or Amma sold them for cash. I didn't know the letters of the alphabet. I felt ashamed to be their sister, though I was excited to see them as well.

I stood on the windowsill on tiptoe and hung on the window bars and anxiously waited for them. When it felt like hours had passed, a car pulled up. Both Aisha and Shati sat in the back with Boro Khala. Wearing a matching dress with shiny shoes, my sisters got out of the car.

I stood by the window without moving when I heard, "Shama."

My sisters were calling for me. We hugged. They wanted me to tell them about Dinajpur and Amma, but I didn't have the words to describe it. Nani stood in the background with a firm look on her face, reminding me to keep my promise, and I did.

It didn't take long for me to feel comfortable again with my sisters. We reunited as if we were never apart. In the absence of both parents, my eldest sister automatically took on the "parent" role and started begging Boro Khala to let me spend the night with them. She agreed, and my sisters helped me pack my overnight bag. I was beyond excited, though I wanted to live at Boro Khala's house with my sisters.

Though they didn't live far from Nani, in Dhaka, a twenty- to thirty-mile drive could take hours due to heavy traffic and congestion in the street. After hours of sitting in traffic, we arrived at Boro Khala's house. She lived on a street filled with government dignitaries. Her neighbors consisted of American ambassadors and foreign officials from throughout the world.

Boro Khala was loved by everyone. She had been taking care of my two sisters like they were her own children. Fairness was very important to her. If she bought an outfit for her own daughter, she made a point to purchase one for my sisters. Her children went to private schools, and with no financial assistance from my parents, she sent my sisters to an expensive school. Her housekeepers didn't want to leave her and called her "Amma." She and my uncle were wealthy, and they shared their wealth generously with others.

My uncle especially built the house for Boro Khala. Before the house was completed, he lost money on a large investment, and the house was never finished. Only the first floor was ready along with a large fountain in the front where flamingoes swam, a garage apartment for their driver and the gardener, and the ground floor for the cooks. The backyard consisted of a swimming pool, tennis court, and a beautiful garden filled with roses and trees.

My sisters took out their books and started trying to teach me. The foundation of the educational system in Bangladesh was laid down during the period of British rule. The system had three levels—primary, secondary, and higher education. Primary and secondary education were both compulsory, though universal participation had remained more an ideal than a fact.

Primary education consisted of eight years while secondary education lasted four years. Secondary education was divided into a lower level and a higher level, and public examinations were held at the conclusion of each level of schooling. Schools in cities and towns were generally better-staffed and better-financed than those in rural areas. Individuals were required to take an entrance exam to qualify for a certain grade level. I knew that I would have to take an exam. I was eight years old, but I didn't know any letters of the alphabet and was terrified to get accepted, and I was terrified to get denied.

My stay at Boro Khala's was only one night. I loved it there. She had two sons and a daughter. Only her eldest son was married to a young woman named Emma. Though barely seventeen years old herself, Emma oversaw all the young kids in the house. She tutored my two sisters and made sure that they were ready for school.

My aunt and uncle's only daughter was fifteen years old. Being born to rich parents, all my cousin's demands and wishes were met. She had her own cook and nanny to look after her special meal requests and her clothing. My cousins lived well and acquired many fancy things. But they also acquired Boro Khala's generous spirit and welcomed my sisters into their home. They did not question my sisters' presence in their home, only accepted them as their siblings. To this day, despite the physical distance, we hold a close bond.

Boro Khala's house had many Western accommodations while Nani's house was modest. At Boro Khala's house, the toilets were upgraded. Her home had showers and flushable toilets. I loved using her fancy bathroom.

Though Nani had indoor plumbing, it was a hole in the ground where human waste accumulated. There was a bucket and a jug for showering. Housekeepers boiled water when you wanted to bathe since there wasn't any hot water. I recall her bathroom to be very slippery where I slid and fell countless times.

I HAD to return to Nani's though, where life was not as easy as it was for my sisters. Nani's middle son was named Dhrobo. In Bengali, the word for uncle is "Mama." So, I called him Dhrobo Mama. During my stay at Nani's, Mama took charge of my education, which meant he got to punish me. Dhrobo was a large built, curly-haired man. He looked different from my other uncles and aunts. And he was like no other. His mood could change in a split second from laughter to rage over the most insignificant of things. The housekeepers feared him, and so did I.

Nani's house had a lot of hired help. A couple of women served as cooks and did household chores, such as laundry and dishes. A young man worked for her as well. He went to the market each day and bought fresh meat and vegetables for our daily meals. He ran errands and did odds and ends around the house. If he showed up from running his errands with even a penny short, my uncle would beat him senselessly.

Mama's eyes always got bloodshot red, and his nostrils would flare when he engaged in his rampant rage. He was big into throwing things, especially shoes. And he didn't discriminate against his target. The housekeepers and drivers were at one point or another beaten by him. I recall the sound of desperation in their voices, as they gasped for air.

The female servants endured most of my uncle's violent rage. The men received his daily verbal abuse; even if they could retaliate, they needed the job, so they never spoke back to Mama. The sound of desperate begging could be heard from every room of the house one afternoon. I stood inside Nani's walk-in closet, hiding, when the door flung open, and a female servant fell to the ground. She kept reaching and grabbing Mama's feet, and she howled and begged. With very little effort, he picked her up off the floor, as her sari unraveled. He kicked her in the stomach, making her fall again. I witnessed this grown woman on the floor, begging for mercy, as he beat her senseless.

"Āmākē kṣamā kara," she screamed, and my uncle just beat her mercilessly until he got tired.

I felt sorry for them. I felt sorry for myself.

I knew that if he were beating on them, I would serve as his punching bag eventually. He spent his days beating, humiliating, and belittling all the women in that house, including Nani, though I did not know why. Nani sat on her bed and prayed all hours of the day. Her prayers grew louder and louder when Mama hit me, but Nani never told him to stop. I didn't understand why this powerful woman did not say stop to my uncle, but I didn't hold a grudge against her.

Nani would just say, "Allah please bring Shamsuddin back, referring to my father, before Dhrobo kills her." And I often wished that he did kill me.

"I am nobody," I say to myself, bending down on my knees, as I had done countless times to say my prayers.

As a form of respect to adults, in Bangladesh, we touched their feet when we said Salam during Islamic holidays or when we saw them after an extended period. It is stated in the Holy Koran that one's heaven rests under our mother's feet. That is why our family observes this tradition of touching feet to ensure a place in heaven.

I bent down to pray five times a day, an Islamic ritual performed by Muslims all over the world. Bending down was our way of demonstrating the complete submission to God, Allah. It was not an act performed by force but acceptance that Allah was the most powerful, the great ruler of all. For me, bending down had no spiritual significance, but I performed dutifully.

But one afternoon, it wasn't God I bent down to kneel before, it was a man. He was the most powerful in my life.

My uncle made me strip down to the bare bones. Perhaps he felt that he needed to humiliate me. But that wasn't the real reason for his anger; it was just an excuse. I felt the Holy Spirit come over me, as he banged my head against the wall. His voice became mute, for I did not need to hear, I needed to only act. I needed to only feel the power of Allah. I needed the Holy Spirit to move me to perform for him.

So, I did. I kneeled not on a prayer rug but on the dirty cemented floor with my arms spread wide lowering my head to him. Without a single word, I kneeled to this man of God and begged for mercy. I knew that my friends couldn't save me from his rage. In utter humiliation and self-loathing, I submitted to him like I never had to Allah. The prayers that I had learned, prayers that I recited each day during my Islamic lessons, all came back to me like an unleashed river of words. I needed to surrender to him. I wanted this for I did not, could not, endure the pain any longer.

Kneeling I repeated, " Āmāra yathēṣṭa śakti nē'i." *I don't have the strength...I don't have the strength.*

I do not know why I gave into my uncle's strength that afternoon since he had overpowered me many times before. It was as if the power of God had moved me like it moved my mother many times when she went into a complete trance. Her body would shake like a fish out of water before it died. I was in a trance, too, but it was not the spirit of God but fear that moved my body.

Mama prayed every day, and on Fridays, he made his journey to the Mosque for a communal submission. I watched him perform the act of powerlessness to God, though he was God in my life. I witnessed him in the most peaceful state and knew that he was capable of compassion.

That day, my head had kept vibrating from the banging when it rose again as if a crane had lifted it up. But it was not a crane; it was his fist gripping a chunk of my hair. My act of submission was not enough for him; he needed more. So, I stripped down to my bare skin, exposing my naked body for him, even though what he desired was my soul. Without a tear on my face, only utter fear, I waited for my penance. He stared me down with his fierce rage, as he spit on the cemented floor. Kicking me back down to my knees, he demanded that I lick his spit off the floor. I hesitated. He spit again aiming a little farther. I realized then that I needed to follow with my tongue like some starved dog in search of spilled crumbs on the floor. So, I did.

It was only the first lick that really mattered. The rest were rituals, and I was well versed with performing rituals for Golam, for God, and now for him. Perhaps his goal was to humiliate me. But it was the act of putting a part of him inside of me, a part that had blended with my own, that haunted me. My saliva and his were one. It ran through my body and resided inside of me. I so desperately wanted to strip down and wash him out, but I did not know how to clean my insides. So, I lived with him. I lived with the evil that he had planted inside of me.

His attacks came quick, as if he had no control of what triggered them. I tried my best to blend in. Always quiet, I stood in the back of the room, busy being invisible. But somehow, he saw me...he would find me as if I were hanging on a rope, just waiting for the punch.

My uncle's insults came in slow motion, as if he wanted me to remember, to feel. He wanted to scar my soul, my heart. And I let him.

"You are unwanted. No one is ever going to come back for you. Your father is never coming back. They are not coming back for you."

He repeated these words, perhaps to hurt me or to not feel alone. At times, I believed him and wept like a hurt, abandoned puppy. At times, I felt anger. The enormous amount of venom and hatred for my mother, Golam, Mama, and God fueled me with strength.

His heavy hands were less painful than his harsh words. At times, I barely endured his metal grip across my face. It cracked my skin as if his fingers ripped through my flesh, leaving his imprint on me. He would wobble, losing his balance, then come at me, weighing down his hand aiming for my face but hitting my head instead. The banging would vibrate my ears as I fell to the ground. I always prayed that I wouldn't land on any object that he could use as a device to further his assault. Landing on his shoes was the worst of my fate. The huge sandals with worn out leather, beaten down from the hours of unpaved streets of Dhaka, would soon come down on me. I could smell the dirt, the filth of the world, as it touched me. His shoes would shatter my shoulder blades, as I gasped for air.

Many times, he would hit me in the stomach with his shoeless feet in a feeble attempt to stop my cry. But the sharp jolt would often cause me to pee uncontrollably. As the urine ran down my legs, I would lay there in pain. The warmth of my urine ironically consoled my bruises and soothed the bitter sting. I would lay motionless, letting him finish.

My unwillingness to fight back, to resist him, would often enrage him even more. But the urine on the floor would disgust him. My urine would make him unclean to perform an Islamic prayer. For his prayers to be accepted by God, he had to perform Wudu, which consisted of cleaning parts of the body that were exposed to dirt and filth. Fearing God would not accept his prayers due to his impurity, he would grab me, pulling me up by my long, dark hair and drag me outside.

The back of my grandmother's flat faced a row of streets vendors. The streets were crowded with people and vehicles of all types. Cars, rickshaws, bikes, and tons of worn-out feet would fill the street of Azimpur. At any given time of the day, you could find groups of men standing, endlessly roaming the streets. To cross into the street, you had to jump across the uncovered drainage system surrounding the flat. I could watch the water and waste flow through the drain. Perhaps it was the city's way of constantly cleaning itself of the sins of its people. The stream seemed endless. On rainy days, the water would flow rapidly. As the water rose, some of the neighborhood kids and I would make paper boats and watch it flow through the streets. We would color our boats to determine the winner of this make-believe race.

That afternoon, however, there were no familiar faces. Strangers watched me, as he made me strip down to my bare skin. I stood there naked, drenched in my urine, completely exposed on display. I could see groups of men gather at a distance. They snickered and laughed and talked about my nakedness. I stood there shivering, unable to defend myself. I stood powerless, as he aimed the hose on me. He was determined to wash me clean and through me, perhaps he would wash his sins. Yet, as the water ran down my body, cleaning me, I felt dirtier than ever. The water tried so hard to wash away the pain of my flesh, but it was unsuccessful. The dirty water bearing his sins would run down the drain. Unlike me, it had an escape.

Perhaps the flow of water soothed his anger. Eventually, he dropped the hose and walked away. I did not question him. I just quickly grabbed my wet clothes and ran into the flat again. Still cold and wet, I bent down and wiped the urine off the floor. My tears created a puddle over my piss, and my soaked body caused the puddle to grow. I cleaned them all as one, for I could not tell them apart anymore.

During bedtime, he would sit on the side of my bed with a belt. As Nani's TV blared, Mama would sit there and watch me "fall" asleep. If my eyelids moved, he would hit my eyelid and yell at me.

"Go to sleep, and stop listening to the TV," he would yell.

I would try my best to lay still and not move. I spent all my energy trying to keep my eyelids from shaking, but often the fear of being hit would make me wet my bed which would send him into even greater rage.

The pressure mounted, as the days got closer to exam day for school. To be admitted, I needed to pass the entrance exam. I studied not only because I wanted to go to school, but the fear of shaming our family should I fail was even greater. Everyone kept asking, "When is Shama starting school; why she isn't in school?" Their questions made me ashamed and embarrassed.

My uncle would sit with a belt or often hold his shoes as he tried to teach me the alphabet. If I got a letter out of order, he would hit my head with his shoes. And if I cried, he would hit me harder. Mama didn't want Nani to hear me crying, so I was punished harder if I cried.

Mama also knew that I loved cats. There were many strays near Nani's flat. I would feed them and pet them whenever I saw one. Mama would chase the cats around and set traps for them. He wanted to always let me know that he was in control.

The day of the entrance exam arrived, and I was terrified, not of the test, but what Mama would do if I didn't pass. I remember walking to school. The headmaster knew Nani well. Nani had made many donations to the school. The moment I walked in, the schoolteachers started saying, "You will have no problem. You are from a distinguished family."

After several hours of testing, most of which I just sat and stared at the page, my exam was over. The grading didn't take since most of the pages were left blank.

The headmaster called Nani and me into her office. She looked at Nani and shook her head. She told her, "Appa, your granddaughter is not smart. You should save your money for her dowry and find her a husband."

I just wanted to die in shame and humiliation. I couldn't think of what Mama would do to me. I could only hear the headmaster's words repeatedly in my mind.

Nani looked at her and said, "Perhaps we can do something." She opened her purse and pulled out a stack of cash.

The headmaster said, "Appa, I just don't know if we can place her."

Nani then asked if I could enter on provisional grounds. If I didn't catch up to my grade level within six months, I could be demoted to a lower grade level. She agreed to that proposition and took Nani's money.

On the way back home, Nani told me that I really needed to study. I would be an embarrassment to our family if I got demoted to a lower grade. I promised her that I would study my hardest. Nani and I stopped and bought my school uniform. I had been dreaming about school uniforms for years, and finally, I was about to enter school. I couldn't wait to show my imaginary friends the school uniform.

My uniform consisted of a white, short-sleeved shirt and a navy-blue skirt. We had to wear closed-toe shoes with white socks. We had strict uniforms, and daily, our outfits were inspected for compliance.

All kids were required to bring lunch from home. Since there was no public school in Dhaka, everyone who attended school had the means to pay for their education. Agrani was the school that was close to Nani's house in Azimpur and where I was accepted to attend.

Since the schools were based on British school systems, I was accepted into the primary level schooling. Agrani was a Bengali school where Bengal was the school's primary language. An English-medium education system is one that uses English as the primary medium of instruction—particularly where English is not the mother tongue of the students. Though my sisters were attending a school that would prepare them for our potential move to the United States unlike me, I was still happy to start my education at the Bengal-language school.

When Nani and I arrived home that day, my uncle asked how I did on the exam. I said nothing but shamefully hid my face.

He jumped up and said, "Well, did you pass?"

Nani said, "Shama was accepted under provisional entrance. She has six months to catch up to her peers, or she will be expelled from school."

My uncle shook his head and said, "You stupid girl. How embarrassing for our family."

Soon all my relatives knew that Nani had to pay and beg for my acceptance. I was beyond ashamed and mortified. I just hoped that Abba didn't find out. I didn't want to disappoint him.

My uncle became even more abusive during my studies. There were times, I could barely see the words on the page straight because my head was spinning from the banging it received from him.

In Bengali, there are two different sets of alphabet. One set of alphabet for consonants and one set for vowels. In addition, I had to learn the English alphabet as well as Arabic to read the Quran. I was good at memorizing, so I learned the letters quickly; however, I could not identify them by sight.

I had accepted that I was not smart. Everyone called me stupid or treated me as such. Comments like, "Well, this is not surprising that you did so poorly on the exam," came from almost everyone. I suspected that they were correct, and I was simply stupid.

Nonetheless I needed to be educated. I wanted to hold a book and know which side was up because I could recognize words. I wanted to be able to read the letters and cards that Abba sent. But mostly, I didn't want to be stupid any longer.

AFTER MOVING BACK TO DHAKA, I would receive word about Abba more frequently than I did when I lived in Dinajpur. We received birthday cards; and when family or friends returned from America, they bought with them a box of candy that Abba sent. There were a couple of times when Abba even called. Getting on the phone with Abba made me very nervous and self-conscious. I was nervous that he may use an English word or phrase, and I wouldn't understand him. He knew that my sisters were going to school, and they were being properly educated. But he didn't know that I didn't even know the letters of the alphabet.

Often, I would lock myself in the bathroom when he called to avoid getting on the phone. Sometimes the connection was so bad that we could barely hear him. Everyone screamed loudly and had to repeat everything several times. Often the call would drop in the middle of the conversation. Abba also sent telegrams if he needed to convey a quick message to us.

The most important telegram came one afternoon at Nani's house. It was from Abba. It read "Tickets purchased...coming to Dhaka on January 3rd".

Everyone took turns to look at the telegram, even those who could not read English. I guess we all wanted to see those words on a piece of paper for ourselves. Telegrams were always brief because there was a word limit, and it could be read by anyone, so nothing too private was shared. On a small piece of paper, some typed letters were all one saw.

Along with excitement, panic settled in when the reality of moving to America became not just a dream but for real. Aisha and Shati started practicing English and worked on various phrases. Nani sent Amma a telegram in Dinajpur stating that Abba was on his way back to Dhaka, and Amma needed to return. A few days passed when we received a telegram response from Amma, stating, "I am not coming. I am not going to America."

My three uncles and two aunts all convened at Nani's house to discuss Amma's telegram. My sisters and

I were in the next room and could hear everything. One of my uncles suggested that they go get Amma. There were several arguments that broke out in trying to figure out the best way to bring Amma in Dhaka prior to Abba's arrival.

They collectively decided that all three uncles along with the three of us girls would go to Dinajpur. If Amma refused to leave with us, then they would leave the three of us there at Golam's compound. My uncles and aunts were certain that once Amma saw her daughters, she would not hesitate to leave Golam.

Nani and everyone told my two sisters and I to pack our suitcases, and we were moving to Dinajpur. My two sisters had no idea what life was like at Golam's compound, but unfortunately, I did.

I started bedwetting again. As the days got closer to our departure for Dinajpur, I took hot water and poured it between my legs. I took witch hazel and mixed it with water and poured it between my legs in fear of the burning sting that I would feel again after Golam got off me.

I pinched and hit myself. I poured hot water down my head to remind myself of the life I lived at Golam's. "I don't want to go back," I told my imaginary friends as they kept telling me that they weren't going to leave me. Though they did not want to go back to Dinajpur, they kept telling me that I wouldn't be returning alone, that they would never leave.

As I think back, I recognize that my options were not great. Either I remained at Nani's, where Mama used me as his punching bag, or I returned to Dinajpur, where I was woken up in the middle of the night by Golam. What I really wanted was for Boro Khala to take me, and I could not find the courage to ask her to save me. Nor could I understand her reasoning for not taking me in the first place when both of my sisters were already living with her. But I knew that if Mama found out that I told Boro Khala about his violent rage, he would certainly kill me. And if I told Boro Khala where I slept at Golam's house, Nani would kill me. So, in the end, it didn't matter where I went. I just needed to survive until Abba came back for me.

At least at Nani's house, I received enough food to eat. I was able to shower and sleep. And I got to see my sisters occasionally. At Nani's, I started to learn to read and write. My life was better; and though my mother seemed indifferent of my whereabouts, I did miss her. I missed our family, especially my sisters and Abba. And I even missed my cat.

The night before we left for Dinajpur, everyone came to Nani's house for a big family dinner. My sisters were crying; they didn't want to leave. Boro Khala was crying and giving us hugs. I still remember sitting on Boro Khala's lap and playing with a ring that she wore often. It was a beautiful gold ring that looked to me like a crown. Imbedded in each layer of the crown-shaped ring were various gems. I always referred to it as Khala's crown. Over a decade later, Boro Khala gifted me that ring which I have saved to give to my youngest daughter.

Our cousins bought parting gifts for the three of us. Silver bangles for each arm were a special gift from Boro Khala. I knew that the moment Golam saw them, he would sell them. I didn't want to wear them, but hide them, except Boro Khala insisted that we wear them, so we could always remember her.

I recall not sleeping much that evening. I remember stuffing myself with various assortments of food, as if I would be able to store it inside of me when I got hungry at Golam's. Early the following morning, my three uncles, two sisters, and I got in a car and headed to Dinajpur. The drive to Dinajpur was long with multiple stops along the way. As the car got closer to Golam's house, my stomach felt woozy, and I wanted to throw up. I was anxious to get there. I wanted it all to just be over.

The anticipation of seeing Amma was filled with mixed emotions. I missed Amma, but I didn't want to live in Dinajpur. *Would my uncles really leave me here with Amma and Golam?* I wondered. My imaginary friends tried their best to distract me, but I just couldn't focus. They pointed out all the beautiful flowers and the large green trees that we passed on the drive. They pointed out colorful saris that hung to dry as they floated freely with the wind, creating a sea of colors. The beauty of Dinajpur was lost in my excruciating memory forever. I could no longer see past my painful experience to appreciate its vast green fields that echoed the sounds of blowing leaves. I could not appreciate the simplicity and depth of its people and culture.

I couldn't focus on anything. I felt sick, and my head felt heavy. I wanted to sink into a long sleep and never wake up. I wanted my imaginary friends to take me away and hide me in the meadows under bushes of daisies. I wanted to fly away like the butterflies that I once chased.

They flew so fast, slowly disappearing into the blue sky. I too wanted to disappear, float away. I wanted to be free.

Our car pulled up to Golam's gate, which was closed. Everything looked the same to me. Our driver honked the horn several times, but no one came out. So, he got out of the car and yelled "Daraja khola." (Open the door.) Still, no sign of anyone. Dhrobo Mama got out of the car, and they huddled around to talk. My sisters and I remained quiet and waited for instructions.

Our driver along with my uncles opened the gate with an easy push. The gate was not locked. After the gate opened, everyone got back into the vehicle, and we moved forward. The entire compound looked and felt deserted. There were no signs of a single person. The kids who normally hung from the banana trees, the women who sat by the fire pit, the guards who stood at post—all were gone. The silence felt eerie. I looked for Raja and the other kids, but there was no one.

As I walked through the open corridor, the memories of my life there flooded me. The spot where Raja and I played Hopscotch, the marking on the cement was still there. The tree whose fallen twigs we used as a toothbrush still stood strong. My uncles opened door after door but still no sign of anyone.

He looked at me and said, "Where would they be?"

I could only assume that somehow Golam must have heard that we were coming, so he packed up and abandoned his compound prior to our arrival.

Everything, especially the fact that my sisters, my uncles, and me stood inside Golam's compound felt like a dream. For a moment, I couldn't tell if I was dreaming that they were there with me or if Golam was a dream. Nothing felt real. The imaginary world and reality blended seamlessly, as I stood wondering if I would ever see my mother again.

I knew that Golam's prayer room was the biggest place in the entire compound, so I led everyone there. As we got closer to the room, I could hear a loud moaning coming from inside. My uncle opened the door, and my sisters and I stepped back. Inside the room was Amma, looking disoriented, as if she were in some type of trance. She was laying in the corner with her eyes shut, mumbling words that I could not understand. My sisters hadn't seen her in almost four years and ran to her.

With a smile on her face, my eldest sister said, "Amma, we are here. Look Shati and Shama are here, too."

Amma looked at us, but she did see us. She was lost in her world. With gazed eyes, she stared into space.

My uncle said, "We are here to take you back to Dhaka with us."

Aisha said, "Abba is coming from America."

My mother screamed, "No," and began pushing furniture towards us. My eldest sister almost fell when Amma started screaming. My sisters had never witnessed Amma's rants.

My youngest uncle approached her when my mother began hitting him. Then my mother began banging her head against the wall and panting heavily. All three of us started screaming and crying. Someone directed my sisters and me to get back in the car. We hesitated. We didn't know what to do except plead with Amma to come with us. But she kept banging her head and screaming uncontrollably.

Dhrobo Mama grabbed her and picked her up, as she kicked and hit in attempt to get freed. We all rushed to the car. My uncles tried to restrain my mother, as they shoved her in the car. Amma screamed, but still no one came out. I don't know if the entire place was empty, or people simply hid from us. But the only sound that could be heard was Amma's screams. In the car, Amma banged her head against the car window until she fell unconscious.

We spent that night in Lal Qutie, though none of us slept much. The local doctor made a visit to the house to give Amma sedatives. I wasn't privy to the adults' conversation, so I did not know of our plans. Except the next morning after breakfast, we headed back to Dhaka.

That was the last time that I visited Dinajpur. I never heard from Golam again. No one spoke his name; no one spoke about Amma's life with him. He and the last four years were erased from our memories, or at least, we pretended. I know that I certainly did try to forget.

I was terrified to be around my own mother. She had sudden outbursts and kicked anyone who tried to get close to her. The erratic behavior made me nervous. I did not recognize her and knew that it was even more difficult for my sisters. No one spoke; we just sat in the car in silence afraid to speak. I wondered why my mother loved Golam more than me. Why she didn't miss her daughters. Why she didn't grab and hug me when she saw me. But mostly, I wondered what was wrong with me.

THE LONG DRIVE ended at Nani's house, where I'd been living. Amma, though less than five feet tall and frail, kicked and screamed with all her might. My uncles forced her out of the car, as they tried to usher her into the house. Amma didn't want to move. She didn't care that she created a scene or that a crowd of strangers had gathered to watch. She screamed to an exhaustion and again lost consciousness.

That day outside of Nani's house, I watched my sisters witness her rants for the first time. I recognized that fear in their eyes. I had forgotten how it felt to witness it for the first time. I thought that Amma had died that first time I saw her faint. But on that day, I wished that she did die.

I have witnessed countless times, where Amma lost consciousness, and I no longer feared her theatrical performance. Video clips of young girls at The Beatles' concerts, screaming and fainting, reminded me of my mother and the other women, as they fell on Golam's feet. His presence and his words somehow moved them to lose consciousness. Amma often laid on the floor breathing heavily, as she moved her head nonstop from left to right. After witnessing several episodes of this display of adornment, I became accustomed to it. I was amused by it. Their display of emotions felt inauthentic and forced, as if they were possessed by some demons.

My uncles wasted no time and quickly lifted her and carried her inside. The housekeeper locked the door behind us and stood around not knowing what to do.

Amma, like a kidnapped woman, pleaded to escape. She wanted to be with Golam. She wanted to be anywhere else except with us. Thankfully, all Amma's antics caused her to be drained and exhausted. And like a small child after a tantrum, she too fell asleep and was carried to a bed. No one conveyed a plan, certainly not to me, on what do to when she woke up.

Nani just muttered, "Allah, let Shamsuddin come and take them away to America," as her fingers stroked a string of beads.

Boro Khala came to visit and seemed relieved to see us, especially both Aisha and Shati. And she took them back to her place while I remained with Amma and Nani.

Amma came in and out of consciousness, and each time, she uttered words, which seldom made any sense. She spoke in tongues and paced around the house until she passed out. Each time she woke, she screamed loudly and cried. Amma's bed laid next to Nani's, and I slept in a cot in between the two beds. Amma was almost barricaded in the center, though it did not deter her from trying to escape.

As the night grew late, I drifted off to sleep. The sudden sounds of banging and footsteps woke me. Dhrobo Mama stood in the front of the door guarding it while Amma kicked and tried to push her way out.

Soon the rest of the house woke, as everyone tried to calm Amma. But nothing seemed to work, and she ran around the house throwing pots and pans at him and anyone who came near her. More screaming broke out, as Dhrobo Mama became agitated. He grabbed the coffee table and raised it up, as if to throw it at her. Both Nani and I screamed. He threw the table down, only inches away from Amma and walked away. I still remember the rage in his eyes, and for once I didn't blame him. We were all exhausted from Amma's nonstop screaming rants.

I sat in a corner of Amma's bed, not knowing what to do. I wanted to ask her why she didn't want to be with us. I wanted her to choose us over Golam. I wanted to ask her so many things. Instead, I just sat next to her like a stranger with only one thing in common—our inability to feel. We sat, for how long I don't remember, except that exhaustion consumed me. We sat with a gaping distance between us that physical closeness would never fill.

As days went by, Amma remained committed to escape. Only Nani and my uncles came in and out of the house. During that period of her initial reentry, my sisters barely came to Nani's place. I was on watch duty with instructions to let someone know if Amma tried to escape. I did not return to school. Watching Amma was more important. Perhaps it was deemed unnecessary for me to go to school since our plans to move to America became more real with each passing day. I would have loved to attend school and get away from the craziness of each day with Amma.

The doctor paid many house visits to check on Amma and to give her sedatives. It became a part of our daily routine. I hated being responsible for keeping track of her. I didn't want to spy on her. I hated having to give reports back to my uncles each day even more. We didn't celebrate Amma's return with a big family feast. We never really talked about her absence from our lives. We never talked about Dinajpur. The past no longer existed, only hope of Abba's return to Dhaka and our new life in America.

The sun seldom gave us a break from the scorching heat. People simply learned to adapt. Afternoon naps served as a retreat from the heat. Often the midday quietness felt endless. No loud noise, only the sound of the fan could be heard throughout the house. Boredom consumed me like many young kids my age refusing to take a nap.

I looked up and saw Amma signaling me to get up and follow her. I did.

She and I walked quietly out the front door into the street where she motioned a rickshaw. "Amma, we aren't supposed to go anywhere," I told her.

"Quiet," Amma replied and pinched my arm in a familiar way. Anytime I didn't behave to her or Golam's liking, Amma pinched me.

Amma valued Shashab's opinions and sought his guidance. So, she flagged a rickshaw, and the two of us got in. The driver paddled swiftly through familiar roads. I gripped the handlebar tightly. as cars swarmed around us. There was nothing holding us inside the rickshaw, no seatbelt, nothing. And if it stopped without much notice, you had to grab the side bar to keep yourself from falling out. Dhaka streets weren't for the faint of heart. At times, I would simply close my eyes and pray until we passed unsafe situations.

I no longer wanted anything to do with Shashab, Golam, or any self-proclaimed holy man. I hated Shashab and Golam. I hated the power that they had over my mother. I hated that she loved them more than us. I hated that in their presence, her daughters meant nothing to her. Being in a room with Golam or Shashab only validated that my mother was capable of love. She just didn't love her children and undeniably regretted giving birth to throwaway girls.

Shashab looked aged since the last time I had seen him, almost four years ago. His house was still packed with his followers who brought him gifts and food in hopes of his blessings. The moment he saw Amma enter, he told everyone to leave the room. Amma ran to him like long lost lovers finding each other again. She touched his feet and began crying. I couldn't tell if her tears were of joy to be in his presence or tears of sadness that her family forcefully brought her back to Dhaka. Shashab stroked my mother like a child and guided her up to standing. They sat on the floor over a big hand-stitched quilt and spoke. I wasn't privy to Shashab and my mother's conversations. I sat at a distance, trying my best to read the expressions on their faces. Amma kept bowing down, and he stroked her back like a parent to a small child.

Shashab stood up and said to Amma, "You need to go and be with your husband and your family. I am instructing you to be a wife and a mother."

Tears ran down my mother's face, as she nodded her head in acceptance of his instructions. She and I got in a rickshaw and headed back to Nani's house.

Upon arrival at Nani's house, we found everyone up from their nap and panicked. The quietness that filled that house soon came to an end, as Amma and her brothers screamed and shouted.

Amma didn't try to go see Shashab again. Perhaps his instructions to her to be a mother and wife deterred her or perhaps the fighting and threats from her brothers deterred her. She reluctantly accepted her life and didn't demonstrate a lot of enthusiasm about moving to America or about Abba's arrival.

Though she didn't try to escape, I found myself still "keeping my eyes" on her and reported back to my uncles or Nani if I thought she did anything suspicious. At times, I felt guilty for tattling, but I knew that she couldn't be trusted. I also knew that the more I tattled on her to my uncles, the more they liked me and would hit me less.

Once Amma pulled out some of her gold jewelry. I became fearful that she may sell the pieces to buy a bus ticket back to Dinajpur, so I ran and told my uncles. Afterwards, Nani locked up all Amma's valuables in her cabinet. Amma frantically looked for them without knowing that Nani had put them away for safekeeping. I didn't dare tell her that I knew where Nani hid her jewels.

As the days got closer to Abba's arrival, no one worried if I studied or not. Everyone just anxiously waited for Abba's arrival. "Am I really moving to America?" I wondered to myself as I looked at my paper dolls and wondered if people really had golden hair and white skin. The excitement of moving to America did not lessen my fear of learning and speaking English. It terrified me.

Boro Khala decided that my sisters and I needed some nice matching dresses for America. She purchased fabrics and had a tailor make dresses for us. I loved getting a ribbon made with any extra fabric for my long hair. My hair was finally growing long after it had been shaved several times by Mama after moving back to Dhaka because of head lice. Amma often told me that long hair on girls was appealing to traditional Muslim men, and it would help me to find a husband.

My older cousins, who had travelled abroad and knew the Western way of life, began to give us a fast course on how to eat with forks and knives. In Bangladesh, rice, dal, everything, we ate with our fingers. At restaurants, individuals used forks and other utensils, but young kids seldom went out to eat at restaurants.

My rare attempts to eat with a fork ended in disaster. I dropped food and could never figure out how to cut meat. Normally I left the restaurant still hungry rather than embarrassing myself trying to eat with a fork.

My cousins set the table with empty plates and lined up forks, spoons, knives, and even napkins. We learned how to place the napkin on our lap. Then my sisters and I picked up each utensil and practiced holding a pretend piece of meat down with a fork then cutting the meat using a knife. I always wanted to be the last to start eating, so I could watch others. I never asked for seconds since eating with utensils was so stressful. My sisters learned a lot faster, especially since they watched kids use utensils at their school.

For days, we practiced, and afterwards, all of us went out to a Chinese restaurant to eat dinner. I had butterflies in my stomach. My cousin sat across from me, and I followed her lead. Each time she picked a utensil, I followed suit. I don't know if I enjoyed the meal since all of my focus went to the art of eating.

The day finally arrived, after almost five years of separation, our father was returning. The excitement consumed not only me and my sisters but our entire extended family. Everyone prepared as if a big wedding or a soccer match was about to take place. My sisters and I rushed around, giggling, as we put on our pink satin dresses, black leather shoes, and white socks. I still recall that dress with three shades of pink, one of my favorites. The lightest shade of pink was on top, and the darkest shade of pink landed right above my knee. My hair pulled back with a matching pink ribbon. I felt like royalty, a princess. The entire family which included my uncles, aunts, and cousins all headed to the airport to pick up Abba.

Amma, my sisters, and I moved into Boro Khala's house for the remainder of our time in Dhaka. Nani's place couldn't accommodate our entire family, but Boro Khala had a larger house. My cousins had to make some big sacrifices. They gave up their room and moved into the den while the housekeepers got my parents' room prepared for Abba's arrival.

The drivers lined up the cars, as everyone began to file in. The drive to Dhaka airport consisted of various detours and unpredictable delays. We had no time to waste. As I rushed to get into a vehicle, Nani motioned me over to her.

I walked up to her, and she grabbed my arm and pulled me aside.

Quietly she said, "Never tell you father where you and your mother slept. Never tell him those things, or he will not take you to America. You will bring shame to your family. Never speak a word of it to anyone."

I nodded yes and promised her that it would remain a secret. Her demeanor and request felt strange and confusing to me.

Why would she mention Dinajpur? Was there something weird with what took place there? I thought to myself.

As I walked back to where my sisters stood, my eldest sister Aisha asked, "What did Nani tell you?"

I replied, "Not to tell anyone where Amma and I slept in Dinajpur."

I never discussed that incident or our sleeping arrangements in Dinajpur again and kept my promise to Nani.

But as years passed, I never forgot that very moment of secrecy. It was much later in life that I began to understand the reasoning behind her request. Nani wanted to protect Amma and my parents' marriage. She feared Abba's reaction should he ever find out about Dinajpur. That incident outside of Boro Khala's house when Nani asked me to keep a secret planted a seed inside me. I began to wonder if there was something wrong with what I witnessed and experienced at the hands of Golam and my mother. I began to understand that Golam climbing on top of me, and my mother's compliancy was secret-worthy, a shameful secret at that.

I knew that only Amma and I would carry that secret to America. It would be ours to keep for the sake of our family. Though she and I never spoke about what took place in Dinajpur, I reminded her of her past. A past that if found out could destroy our family and more importantly hurt Abba. To this day, I regret that I never confided in Abba. I did not tell him the truth to not just protect my family, but to protect myself. I was certain that he would disown me. I carried that shame into my adulthood.

4. The Secret

From a distance, our long procession of cars emulated a presidential motorcade. That day had all the makings of a once in a lifetime moment. Motorcade or not, my father had all the presidential qualities. He alone held our future in his hands. I didn't care if he worked as a janitor or a businessman back in the States. That day at Dhaka International Airport, a presidential-type figure was scheduled to arrive. That figure, my father, had the power to change the course of our lives.

I vacillated from excitement and sheer fear as we waited at the terminal. Each time an airplane de-boarded, I watched people walk down steep stairs off the plane and into the airport. Families gathered to greet their loved ones. But mostly, I watched tall, white men in matching shirts walk inside, towering over all of us. Rescue workers and medical personnel from various organizations abroad arrived in Dhaka in an attempt to provide humanitarian services. Though the war had ended several years earlier, the devastation that Bangladesh endured felt beyond recovery. These foreigners came to put a bandage on our bleak future.

I feared that I wouldn't recognize my father, but mostly I feared that Abba wouldn't recognize me. What if he starts speaking in English with me? How will we communicate? These last five years passed slowly, and with each day, memories of him faded. I often wondered if he really existed or if I had invented him to simply ease my mind.

The real and the imaginary, both equally dominated my mind, and at times, I found it difficult to discern. Everyone made fun of me for walking around and talking to myself. Sometimes cousins, even uncles, quietly followed me, so they could listen in my conversation with my imaginary friends.

Abba had been so real to me that I felt his arms around me when he hugged me; his strength covered me, and I could smell him throughout the day as if the meadows followed me wherever I went. In these past five years, however, as Abba drifted further and further away, my friends came closer into my life.

We all hovered over this large window in the crowded airport. I could see from a distance an airplane landing.

Someone yelled, "That is British Airways."

My heart pounded. Abba's flight had just landed. Nausea from excitement and nervousness all filled my stomach. I kept getting shoved away from the window and didn't see the plane tarmac to the gate. I just saw people filed in a long line, some holding signs for any

Westerners getting off the plane. We stood there with the masses. I didn't look for Amma; my eyes were focused on the door. Tall figures blocked my view, so I stood on my tiptoes and stared. A guard approached the locked door and opened it. More people pushed and shoved to get a view. I hadn't experienced such a crowd. It felt like everyone from Dhaka was at the airport that afternoon. One after another, folks de-boarded the airplane.

My tall cousin got the first view of Abba and yelled, "Shamsuddin Bhayi. Shamsuddin Bhayi."

This bald, pudgy man with thick glasses didn't seem to hear and kept walking towards the door.

Others began to get his attention, "Shamsuddin Bhayi," they yelled louder.

He finally looked up and waved. That man in the distance resembled a man I once knew; my father had returned from the States, like he told me that he would.

Abba barely made his way out the door before a crowd of relatives circled and engulfed him.

I could no longer see him when Boro Khala looked at me and said, "Go give your Abba a hug."

I hesitated. This man dressed in brown slacks that was held up by this worn-out belt with a plaid shirt and rolled up sleeves tucked inside his pants looked disoriented from exhaustion.

Abba barely had any hair, the sun reflected from his forehead. His horn-rimmed glasses slid over his nose, as drops of sweat ran down his face. His chin looked familiar. I saw it every time I looked in the mirror. People told me that I looked like him, and today for the first time, I knew why.

Carrying his hard, shell silver briefcase, Abba approached us. He gave my two sisters and me a hug and asked, "How are your studies?"

Gulp, I was afraid to answer, but fortunately the crowded airport didn't allow us the opportunity to have a conversation. The crowd pushed and shoved us apart once again.

I wanted Abba to meet my friends. For five years, I had been telling them about Abba. I scanned the airport, but I could not spot them. *I hope Abba likes my friends*, I thought to myself as I moved with the crowd.

The security line to pass inspection at Dhaka airport, especially after the Independence War, took a long time. The process was grueling and could take hours. Fortunately, we had some family connections working for airport security that allowed Abba to cut through the inspection swiftly with his luggage. Once outside the airport, we packed into the caravan of cars and headed back to Boro Khala's house.

I don't recall where my sisters sat, but I rode with Amma and Abba in the backseat. My youngest uncle sat in the front with the driver. The two of them spoke, and at times, Abba joined in.

The roads to Boro Khala's house seemed to take forever with the busy traffic. Abba made comments about Dhaka's traffic, but every statement followed with, "Wait until you see the road in America. People drive fast. There are no cows or rickshaws there. On roads called the highways, all you hear is cars, and the sound of the engine; no one honks; and women drive, too. Maybe, you girls will learn how to drive one day."

His words were so far from my reality that I couldn't visualize what he was telling us. A part of me still wasn't convinced that we were going to America. Amma looked disinterested and distanced from Abba. He didn't seem to be phased by her reaction. It is not uncommon for a man and a woman to not show any affection in public. So, my parents' interaction with each other was not uncommon.

We walked inside Boro Khala's house to find her long, glass dining table filled with a variety of Bangla dishes, enough to feed an entire village. The fragrance from the variety of curry dishes filled up the room, and my stomach growled with hunger. The excitement of Abba's arrival mixed with nervousness had my stomach in knots for days, but now my nerves had settled. I couldn't wait to feast on the countless assortment of dishes.

My aunt's big house with an open floor plan allowed our large family to gather at meal times. My uncles, aunts, cousins, even the housekeepers swarmed Abba. All excited to hear about life in America. But before we could start eating, Abba opened his suitcase and took out gifts for everyone. Boxes after boxes of chocolates, some in tin boxes and some cardboard boxes. They all looked beautiful, too pretty to rip open. Even his suitcase smelled of America, fresh fragrant, something totally unfamiliar to me. Everything, including his clothes, felt cold as if they had been stored in a refrigerator. I picked up a few of his clothes and took a deep breath. Everything looked new and crisp.

Even his shaving cream, shampoo, all looked so beautiful and nicely packaged. Abba handed me a big box of chocolates with cellophane wrapping and asked me to share with everyone. I frantically unwrapped to find not one but three layers of candy that I couldn't decide how many I could fit in my mouth at once. He gave my sisters some beautiful silver bracelets and me, paper dolls. I took my gift and ran to find a safe place to hide them like I did in Dinajpur. I wanted to make sure that my presents remained safe and not confiscated like many times before in Dinajpur.

The evening grew late, and Abba's jetlag made him tired, so reluctantly folks began to leave. Both Aisha and Shati went off in our cousin's room, and I with my parents. As I got ready to sleep, I heard Abba say to Amma, "I don't care what you did that is between you and Allah. It is not for me to forgive. I just want a new beginning from this point forward."

I didn't know if Abba had any idea that Amma and I had lived in Dinajpur. I didn't know if Abba knew of Golam. I just knew that I needed to keep my promise to Nani and never tell Abba where we slept. I didn't want to disappoint Abba. I didn't want him to leave me behind in Bangladesh and return to America. So, I said nothing to him.

The first night after Abba arrived in Dhaka, I slept with him and Amma, like I did with Golam and Amma. I recall getting in bed feeling nervous and wondering why Aisha and Shati didn't have to sleep with us. As the room got dark, Abba reached over and put his arms over my shoulder, then he stroked my head. Golam never expressed that type of affection towards me. I waited for Abba to climb on top of me except he fell asleep and shortly after began to snore loudly. The following night and many more after, Abba simply gave me a hug and drifted off to sleep.

Amma insisted that Abba visit Shashab and have him bless our move to America. To satisfy Amma, Abba agreed. I did not accompany them to Shashab's place. Abba sometimes humored Amma's wishes. He did not believe in such "spiritual" leaders. He called them phony but knew it was important to Amma.

After returning from visiting Shashab, Amma said that she had a premonition that some incident will keep us from getting plane tickets.

"I have a feeling that something will keep us from leaving," she said.

Amma was always very superstitious and often negative. For whatever reason, I feared her words. I feared that she would be right, and we would remain in Dhaka.

Abba said nothing and listened to Amma. I just wanted her to shut up. She had a way of ruining any chance of happiness for us. But that didn't keep Abba from having a big grin on his face. He simply opened his briefcase and took out five plane tickets with each of our names on it. We all screamed with excitement. I held the airline ticket in my hand and kept looking at my name. Though I could barely read at all, I knew that this piece of paper held my family's future.

Amma insisted that we won't get a visa. Her insistence made me nervous and anxious. I didn't want her to sabotage this for us. "What if Amma is right? What are we going to do?" I asked my friends. And they kept reassuring me to have faith in Abba. Many times, my friends and I sat and imagined life in America and if Memphis looked the same as Walnut Grove. Would we have a little house like Laura Ingalls, too?

Though Amma believed that our trip was cursed, we began packing. Packing for a family of five to permanently move overseas came with its own challenges. We had limited space, though that didn't keep our relatives from giving us gift after gift to take with us. My sisters and I didn't have any pants, so we packed our dresses knowing that the temperature in March was normally rather cool in Memphis. The temperature in Dhaka never got too cold. Handmade sweaters kept us warm during chilled days in Dhaka.

Boro Khala gave the three of us matching silver bangles, and my younger aunt gave me a jade turtle pendant that I wore to keep them close to me. Our entire life's possessions fit into two large suitcases, ready to relocate. We had no room to pack my toys, but Abba kept telling me about the abundance of toys in America. He promised to take me shopping once we arrived in Memphis.

Almost everyone we knew came to the airport to say their goodbyes. Everyone cried, some because they were going to miss us and some because they were so happy for us. Just knowing about the move to America made me feel special. I knew that it was such an honor to go to America and that so many eagerly waited for such a privilege.

Before boarding the airplane, Nani again reminded me to keep my secret. She pulled me aside and gave me a big hug, making my small head almost lost in her bosom. Her white sari rubbed against my face and wiped away my tears. Nani cried. I don't know if she felt relieved that we were finally going to America or that my uncle's beatings did not kill me. I recall telling her that it will be our secret. I decided that whatever took place in Dinajpur needed to be forgotten and never be discussed. A new beginning waited for us; I just needed to forget the past in order to embrace my future.

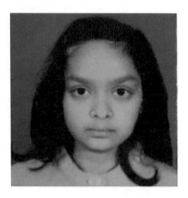

My passport photo

I felt sorry for my friends at Golam's compound. Unlike me, they didn't have Abba to rescue them.

A bus took us close to the airplane. I had never seen an airplane so close before and certainly had never boarded one. I turned around to look at the window, where my relatives stood with their noses pressed against the glass to get a last glimpse before we disappeared into the dust of clouds.

Abba led the way, and we followed onto a small stairway where individuals formed a straight line and entered the doorway of the airplane to escape. Abba, Aisha, Shati, me, and Amma, one by one, we entered this tunnel like space with seats. Abba stopped at our designated seats and told my sisters and me where to sit. It was a cushion seat, nothing too fancy. My sisters and I argued who would sit in the window seat. Abba quickly ended our disagreement and said that we will change planes three times, so each of us could take a turn. Aisha sat by the window from Dhaka to London; London to New York, Shati took a turn; and finally, from New York to Memphis, where our new lives started, I sat by the window on that flight. Regardless of who was by the window, the flight attendants treated the three of us, especially me, like we were special guests.

After we boarded, I met the pilot, though I was too shy to look at him. He handed me a pin with wings and a red zippered bag. We sat back into our seat as Abba and the flight attendant helped my sisters and I buckle our seatbelts. Abba helped Amma who looked anxious and filled with fear.

A mixture of emotions consumed me, and tears of joy and sadness ran down my face uncontrollably. The loud sound of the airplane hid my whimper, and it slowly moved like a gigantic car, making its way past the long row of windows. Though we couldn't see anyone, we knew that they were there waving. So we waved nonstop until we faded into the clouds.

We were all completely dependent on Abba. He was the only one who spoke English since my sisters only knew a few English sentences. So, Abba spoke to the flight attendant regarding our meals. They bought us food to eat in little trays. Everything wrapped nicely, even the forks, knives, and spoons. It all looked too good to eat. Abba said that I could have a can of Coke if I wanted. I never had Coke before; it was only for grown-ups. But on that flight, I drank my first Coke and burped as my nose tingled, and my eyes watered.

I knew only two English sentences when I boarded that plane: First, "My name is Shama." Second, "I don't eat pork." I said those sentences to the flight attendant several times, and she smiled as if she already knew.

The food tasted bland, not the typical spicy taste that we were accustomed to eating, so we added salt and hot sauce to everything we ate. After the meal, the cabin lights turned off.

It had been several hours since we boarded, and yet my sisters, mother, and I hadn't gone to the bathroom. I was too afraid to use the bathroom, and I could only assume that so were my sisters and mother. Abba took each of us, one by one, and showed us how to flush, how to lock the door, and how to wash our hands.

The flight from Dhaka to London was over sixteen hours, so we prepared ourselves for a long night. Abba rented headphones for us, so we could watch movies. I didn't understand English but enjoyed watching colorful cartoons until I drifted off to sleep.

As hours passed, I no longer knew if it was day or night. The time change and the long flight made me completely disoriented. We woke up with the sound of the flight attendant speaking on the intercom.

Abba looked at us and said in Bangla, "We are about to land in London. We are halfway there."

The Heathrow Airport was the largest thing that I had ever seen. It was clean, well lit, and busy. For the first time in my life, I was surrounded by Westerners—people with golden color hair and white skin. I couldn't help but stare. Everyone looked so different.

My sisters and I huddled together and followed Abba's lead.

Our flight from London to New York was delayed, and we needed to spend the night in London. It was already late, and the five of us were exhausted. We huddled inside while Abba waited outside to flag a cab. As the cab pulled up, Abba motioned us to come out. The cold March breeze sent chills up my legs. I shivered as smoke came out of my mouth. We had no jackets, so my sisters and I just quickly rushed into the cab. Abba sat in the front with the driver while we sat in the back.

Exhausted, we all collapsed at the hotel. When I woke up, I didn't know where I was. We hurried and got dressed and headed for breakfast. All through the flight from Bangladesh to London, we were served Bengali food. In London, I ate my very first Western meal. Scrambled eggs and an English muffin were my first Western breakfast items. The eggs tasted bland to me. We were also served fruits. There was always a shortage of apples in Dhaka. By the time we were able to purchase some fruit, it would be highly bruised. I never ate cantaloupe or honeydew in my life, so I was excited to try, but I was hesitant to eat strawberries. The waiter had a funny accent. He was nice and smiled a lot. Our table setting was filled with various utensils. I only knew how to use a fork; and if there was a big piece, I just chewed off a piece at a time. We ate like we had never eaten in our lives.

After breakfast, we boarded our next flight to New York. I heard a lot about the Statue of Liberty and Ellis Island from Abba and was excited to finally see it. Our flight again was very long. As we got closer to America, we were more of a minority on the plane and at the airport. I stared, though Abba kept telling me to stop. I had never seen so many different hair and eye colors. Everyone looked so beautiful to me.

By the time we arrived in New York, we didn't know what day it was or what time. Our nights and days blended after thirty-plus hours of being in transit. I was completely disoriented and filled with excitement. The mere landing on American soil was exciting. The temperature in New York was cold. We were shivering all over. Between our nerves and the chilly wind, we felt cold like never before. We had very little time in New York before heading to our destination, Memphis.

On March 3, 1978, late in the evening, our plane touched down at Memphis airport. Abba called a cab, and we headed for our new home.

It was late at night when our cab pulled up in front of Mrs. Reynolds's house on Rembert Street. Abba rang the doorbell, and we were greeted by Ms. Bell and her big smile. I didn't understand what she said to us except I remember her smile.

A stern woman with pointy glasses and reddish-gray hair that she had styled each week was the owner of the house where Abba rented a room. Mrs. Reynolds, we called her, wore heavy stockings, black laced-up shoes, and skirts. She held her purse with a tight grip and spoke loudly. Her boarders, including Abba, provided her with some extra cash and company, I suppose.

Her home was in a quiet neighborhood, full of mid-size homes. I recall sitting on the porch and swinging. I enjoyed the quietness. Mrs. Reynolds loved decorating her front door. The evening of our arrival, the front door was decorated with colorful eggs, which I found to be rather strange.

Some of the other borders were Ms. Bell, Charlie, and Sammie. Ms. Bell was the caregiver. She looked after everyone. Charlie was blind; Sammie was a disabled veteran; and Abba was working and saving to bring his family to the States.

We were all exhausted from our long journey. Ms. Bell spoke with Abba and began to make room for my two sisters and me to sleep. She moved some cushions from a couch and pulled on a metal bar. The next thing I knew she pulled out a bed like some magic trick. My sisters and I climbed in and went to sleep immediately.

Next morning after breakfast, they called our entire family to the main dining room. When we walked in, we saw that the dining room table was filled with household items from kitchen sponges to trash cans, from towels to bed sheets.

Ever since they heard that Abba was saving money to bring his family to America, they had been purchasing and collecting items for us. I had never witnessed such expressions of generosity until that moment.

Ms. Bell had short, white hair and wore a dress and glasses. I don't recall ever seeing her in pants. She always had on stockings and laced-up shoes. Her pale white skin matched her hair. She was Abba's closest friend and confidant. Ms. Bell looked after Abba and helped him prepare for our arrival.

Charlie was blind and always carried a walking stick. His eyes were glazed over, so I never knew if he was talking to me or not. He touched his food when he ate which made me relieved. If I didn't know how to cut or eat something, I just ate like Charlie.

Sammie, a disabled veteran, seemed distant or perhaps just distracted. Ms. Bell always made sure that Sammie had enough to eat. She was loud. I don't know if she had a hearing problem, but she always screamed. She seemed strict but kind, too. None of them were wealthy people, but they began collecting whatever they could in order to support Abba and our family to start over. I knew that I was surrounded by kind people, and I knew that I wanted to be like them.

It was too late in the school year for us to start school, so for the next several weeks my sisters and I just hung around the house while Abba went to work. On weekends, we looked for a bigger place to rent. Soon Easter holiday was approaching. It was a celebration I had never experienced. Growing up in a Muslim country, Easter is not a part of our tradition. Ms. Bell gave me a chocolate bunny, a beautiful bunny with a little colorful bouquet of flowers. Staring at this gorgeous bunny, I knew that I could not eat it. It was simply too beautiful to eat, so I saved my bunny for months until it had mildew.

I thought when Nani had rescued me from Golam's compound that I was safe. But Mama made sure that I was not. They all made sure that I felt like I was nothing. But here, in America with Abba, I felt safe for the first time in my life. Even though our family owned little as far as material objects were concerned, I didn't worry about someone climbing on top of me or hitting me. All I had to do was learn at school.

5. South Morrison

fter being turned down at numerous apartment complexes, we finally got an interview with a landlord. Most places didn't want to allow three girls below the age of fifteen living at their complex. Perhaps they thought that my sisters and I would be too noisy, and other tenants would complain.

My sisters and I got dressed along with our mother and headed to meet with our potential landlord. Only after a few minutes, they agreed to let us move in. None of us spoke any English, except for Abba, so I guessed we seemed to be very quiet and obedient girls, which we were.

The idea of moving into our own place was very exciting to all of us. Amma would have a full kitchen to cook, and we would have our own television. 50 South Morrison was our very first address in America. It was a two-story house converted into an apartment complex. Downstairs there were two separate tenants. The third door led upstairs. On the top floor there were three doors.

The door on the far left was a single room. It served as my sisters and my bedroom at night, and during the day, it was our living room. The door in the middle had a separate tenant. The door on the far right led to my parents' bedroom, small bathroom, and kitchen. From the kitchen, there was a small balcony and stairs that went downstairs to the trash bins.

We had more space, but I didn't like the idea that a stranger separated my sisters and my room from my parents' room. In the middle of the night, if we needed to use the restroom, we had to walk down the hall.

Since we didn't have any furniture, the landlord let us rent his stuff. In our bedroom, there was a metal framed bed, a small sofa bed, a cheap looking green vinyl couch and loveseat and a coffee table. My parents had a bed and a dresser that held our only television. We didn't own a car, so we purchased a rolling cart to carry our groceries and also used it to take dirty clothes to the Laundromat each week.

We either walked or took the bus. Abba rode the bus every day to and from work at a marble factory where they made marble ashtrays and other knick-knacks, and Abba's job was to ensure that the items didn't have any obvious flaws. I recall looking out my window every evening and watching for him to walk up our street.

The kitchen consisted of a small table with five chairs with mismatched vinyl seats, a sink, and a couple of counters for preparing our meals. Amma loved to cook, though my sisters and I preferred frozen American tray dinners. It was such a treat to eat non-Bengali food. And we ate like we had been starving all our lives. Loaves after loaves of bread were consumed by my sisters and me. The soft, fresh bread with a delicious smell, we couldn't get enough.

Amma saved everything. Every egg carton, jars, and even tin cans. Our kitchen was overflowing with stuff because Amma could not imagine just throwing them away. So, Abba decided that it was time for a trip to the local grocery to show us that there were plenty, and we could buy more. Walking into Kroger's for the first time was overwhelming. Shelf after shelf of nicely packaged items, the stacks of egg cartons, cans of soup—we found ourselves walking with our mouths open in complete awe. After that trip, it was easier for Amma to throw away cartons and other trash.

Like he promised, Abba took me shopping for dolls. I walked into Eckerd's Drug Store and saw their toy section. I was so overwhelmed with all the beautiful toys that I couldn't move. Abba bought me a doll with curly hair and beautiful blue eyes. She was 18-inches tall, and her name was Elizabeth.

I got another doll named Sally. She was a squishy doll and wore a bathrobe. I loved shampooing her hair and squeezing her belly to see bubbles. To this day, I have both of those dolls. They remind me of the happy times in my childhood.

Abba started interviewing for jobs that were more in line with his education. He had two master's degrees in economics and statistics, but Abba couldn't find suitable employment. It became difficult to support all five of us with his salary from the marble factory, so Abba started looking for a second job.

He began bagging groceries at Kroger on nights and weekends. Sometimes, I walked to Kroger and played Pac-Man while waiting for Abba to finish. And sometimes, he gave me a shiny quarter that customers gave him for loading their groceries into their cars.

Memphis ISD offered summer school to those kids failing or not speaking English well. So, my sisters and I took six weeks of summer school. I don't remember much except that it was chaotic. Kids didn't pay attention to the teacher, and most of the time teachers just shook their fingers and said something that I didn't understand. From their expressions, it was easy to derive that they were angry.

As the school year approached, Abba enrolled us for the upcoming fall semester. The school district worker placed us in grades based on our ages. We didn't have to take an entrance exam like we did in Bangladesh. I was told that I would be entering fifth grade in the fall of 1978, at the age of ten. Afterwards, Abba showed us how to walk to the local library, where my sisters and I spent most of our days.

I loved checking out books though I could not read the words on the page. The feel of a book in my hand excited me. I would flip page after page and stare at the words.

My favorite books to check out were history books. Abba read the biography of each U.S. president to us; he thought that before we entered school, we should at least know something about all of the American presidents. And in the evenings, Abba would read them to me, and I would practice reading out loud with him.

As the school year approached, my sisters and I started buying school supplies. Lunch boxes, backpacks, paper, pencils, and Trapper Keepers were just some of the items that we purchased. We also needed some pants. I never owned a pair of jeans until that summer of 1978. My first pair of jeans were Jordache with a red velvet heart on my left hip pocket. I loved them. I loved the way they fit and that I didn't have to worry about crossing my legs properly, so no one could see my panties. Wearing pants gave me a new sense of freedom. I also liked that I could wear whatever I wanted to school, unlike in Dhaka where girls had much stricter dress codes than boys.

In 1978, under federal court supervision, many school districts implemented mandatory busing plans within their district. Memphis ISD implemented busing, and I was bused to Roswell Elementary, which was quite a distance from our home.

Abba wrote a detailed letter and handed it to me with strict instructions to show it to anyone if I got lost or scared. The letter basically told anyone that I didn't speak English and gave Abba's contact information in case of an emergency. With my letter in hand, Abba walked me to the school bus stop.

The school bus driver took me to the principal's office. Mr. Adams talked to the bus driver, then read the letter. Mr. Adams was a large, African American man. I hadn't seen many Blacks, so I stared at him with curiosity. He wore a gold watch, and his hair was curly with tiny curls that filled his head. Some of his hair, along with his mustache, was white. He wasn't dressed fancy but very clean and looked like authority. After he finished reading

Abba's letter, Mr. Adams reached over and grabbed my hand. He smiled as if he had been expecting me all along. The entire time I wanted to throw-up.

The hallway was big. I could hear the echo of our footsteps. Mr. Adams and I stood in front of a classroom door decorated with handprints and flowers, and he knocked on the door. Ms. Whithorn was a large, Black woman with a laugh as big as her bosom. With a strong Christian view and a paddle in her hand, she ruled her classroom.

Fifth grade

Ms. Whithorn opened her classroom door and sternly motioned me in. The other kids jumped out of their seats and approached me. Everyone spoke loudly as if I were deaf. They were loudly repeating themselves, like it would help me understand them. My legs trembled.

I needed to hide; the panic was too unbearable. I launched myself at the first empty desk and sat hunched underneath it. For the next several weeks, that tiny enclave under my wooden desk provided a precious safe haven. Ms. Whithorn never asked me to get up. She continued every day with her teaching which made absolutely no sense to me, while I sat folded underneath. I even ate my lunch there.

I was safe under my desk. Plus, I had already spent almost an entire year, hiding under my bed during the Independence War. All the loud noise from the gunshots and bombs terrified me. But I felt protected under my bed and now my desk.

Sometimes the kids left a note on top of the desk for me. I didn't know what it said, but I looked at their drawings. I would draw a smiley face and place it back on top. I attempted to communicate with the outside world without leaving my safe haven. Weeks passed, but Ms. Whithorn still never asked me to sit up.

From underneath my desk, I would watch the other kids laugh and wondered if Ms. Whithorn said something funny. When the other kids laughed, I laughed; I copied their expressions because I desperately wanted to belong.

Over five weeks had passed when one day from the bottom of my desk, I could see that everyone was reaching inside a bag. They each pulled out a small piece of paper and handed it to Ms. Whithorn. She read a word out loud. Each student would recite some English letters.

When Ms. Whithorn smiled and nodded yes, cheers broke out in the class. I felt their excitement. And in the midst of that excitement, I had forgotten that I was afraid.

I cautiously touched the wooden seat behind me. I started then stopped. I started again. No one was looking at me, so it felt safe. Slowly and quietly, with my head ducked, I pushed up and let my bottom rest on the chair. Clenching my seat, I raised my head. Everyone stopped and looked at me. Ms. Whithorn dropped the bag and words spilled out onto the floor. She put her two hands together. There was a loud sound. That sound echoed throughout the room.

I wanted to make friends, but I was still struggling with spoken English. So Ms. Whithorn decided to start a contest between me and the other Vietnamese boy in my class. The boys were assigned to help the Vietnamese student to learn English, and the girls were assigned to me. Samantha was one of the smartest girls in my class and helped tutor me whenever I needed. She along with the other girls spent their lunch hours tutoring me. Our school principal heard of this contest and got involved. He promised that the winners would get to have a party! The competition got even stiffer, but I loved the attention.

My eleventh birthday was around the corner when I begged Amma and Abba to let me have a party and invite my entire class. They agreed. I went to school the following day and told the class that I was having a party at my home that coming Saturday, and everyone was invited. Abba took me shopping and bought me a special dress for my party. My sisters and mother cleaned our apartment and rearranged furniture to accommodate everyone. I remember the countless platters of food from finger sandwiches to samosas that Amma made. We had punch and tried to think of everything that American kids would like to eat.

On my big day, I got dressed up and waited. We kept looking out the window, but no one came, not a single person. I was heartbroken when we decided to walk to McDonald's for my birthday. Ronald McDonald was at the restaurant and paid a special visit to me. The next time I had a birthday party, I was twenty-two years old.

In November of 1979, fifty-two American diplomats and citizens were taken hostage in Tehran. Iranian revolutionaries held them for 444 days. Anti-Arab and Islamic sentiment grew strong in the States. My father with his thick Asian accent and Islamic heritage, living in the heart of the South, could not find suitable employment.

We couldn't understand why people didn't like us since we were not from Iran. In addition, Iranians were Shiite Muslims, and we were Sunni Muslims. Our religious ideology was very different. Abba just told us people were scared, and it wouldn't last long.

Though there was financial hardship, Abba kept telling us to work hard and that we could be anything in America. He believed in the American dream, and like him, I did, too. He took whatever small jobs that he could in order to provide for us. He made survey calls and distributed flyers for some extra cash. We received food stamps for our groceries. When I was young, I did not fully understand the severity of our financial state. Abba had great faith in God and especially in America.

Growing up, I watched so many mothers hand over their young kids to Nani in hopes that their children would get an education in Dhaka. From very early on, my sisters and I knew that education was the key to success, so we studied. We studied like our lives depended on it, and in many ways, it did. And Abba had high hopes for our future. He told everyone, especially the three of us, that with good education, anything was possible in America.

ABBA WAS VERY proud of me and my sisters. He told everyone even the cashier at Kroger's how quick his daughters were learning English. At times, I would act embarrassed, though secretly it made me happy that he was so very proud.

My eldest sister was taking Pre-AP classes, as I entered middle school. Abba finally received paperwork that allowed him to take the American citizenship exam, but he decided that he would wait. We had already been in the States for four years, so one more year, and we too would be eligible.

"We would take the citizenship oath as a family," Abba told us.

In seventh grade, I made the honor roll for the first time, and in the ninth grade, I was inducted into the

National Jr. Honor Society. My sisters were doing well in school as well.

My teacher told the class about an essay contest that was taking place throughout the State of Tennessee. The topic was citizenship. She encouraged all of us to apply and said that she would add two points to our final grade if we submitted. I wrote about our family's journey to America. And at the National Jr. Honor Society's induction, I read my essay during the ceremony. Several months later in the middle of class, Mr. Adams got on the loudspeaker and called me to his office.

I recall the classmates saying, "You are in trouble."

I didn't know what he wanted, so I nervously walked over to see him. As I turned the corner, I saw a group of men in suits talking to my principal.

As I slowly approached them, Mr. Adams said, "Here she is," pointing to me.

One of the men said, "We were so touched by what you wrote." I had no idea what they were talking about when I realized that they were talking about my essay.

That day, I received an American pin and a $250 savings bond. Later, my essay went on to win the Southeast Regional Essay Contest. I regret that I did not make a copy. I just wanted the extra credits and never imagined that I would win.

Abba was always on the front row of every award ceremony. Amma never took part in these types of special celebrations. She didn't come to my Honor Society induction or any award programs. She rarely left the house unless to visit other Bengali families. But I knew that I could count on Abba to be in the front row of the audience. And he was, not just for me, but he was there for all three of his daughters. Watching him smiling, as I walked across the stage, were some of the happiest memories of my childhood.

It took a couple of years, but soon my sisters and I began to assimilate into American society. One day, an Indian-looking man came and knocked on our door. Abba was out, so we hesitated. He introduced himself and spoke some Bangla. It didn't take long for our families to become friends. They had three daughters, though their kids were younger than us, and we began spending a lot of time together. Soon Amma watched their daughters and earned some extra money to help with our bills. I didn't care for their daughters, mostly I was jealous of the attention that Amma gave them and not us. To this day, the Abrahams are an important part of our family.

———

"Abba, I want the type of jacket that you can unzip the sleeves," I told him.

In 1982, ski jackets were the biggest fad at my middle school in Memphis, and that's what I wanted for my fifteenth birthday. So, we scoured the town looking for the perfect jacket, but I didn't mind. I was out with my Abba, the man whom I loved more than anyone.

"Batta, I'll find you the perfect jacket," he told me, and he did.

It was cream colored with burgundy stripes with removable sleeves. I couldn't wait to wear it. Mid-October in Memphis was rarely cold enough for a ski jacket, but I didn't care. I was going to wear my new jacket on my birthday.

My father and me

The following day, I woke up to hear that Abba had been up all night, complaining about indigestion.

"I probably just ate something bad," Abba said with a cigarette in his hand.

"You need to stop smoking," I told him.

"I am fine, Batta, just get me some Sprite."

I did, but I also hid his cigarettes. Abba referred to me either Shammu Mia or Batta as a term of endearment.

Hours passed, and Abba wasn't any better. Finally, he got dressed and said maybe he should go see a doctor. My sisters were at the Laundromat. I called my friend Charlotte, whose mom often gave me rides to school, to see if her mother could drive us. Charlotte's mom picked up Abba and me and dropped us off at Methodist Hospital. After waiting for almost an hour, the clerk told us that his insurance wasn't accepted at that hospital.

"You have to go to Baptist Memorial Hospital," she said without even looking up from her desk.

Since Charlotte's mother had already left, Abba and I took a cab to Baptist Memorial Hospital. At the hospital, we waited over an hour in the waiting room before they called Abba's name.

For the next several hours, I sat alone flipping through magazines. Finally, I saw a doctor talking to the clerk who pointed to me.

The doctor then walked up to me and said, "Your father suffered a severe heart attack. Do you know what a heart attack is?"

I did not.

"How long will it be before we can leave?" I asked.

The doctor replied, "Your father will be here for a while. Do you have a mother or someone you can call?"

Most of the Bengali families that we knew in Memphis were doctors, and they were all out of town at a conference. I called my mother and told her that Abba had a heart attack, and he had to stay at the hospital. I don't know if she even knew the severity of his heart attack; I certainly did not.

Once my sisters returned from the Laundromat, the three of them came to the hospital. My sisters called our close family friends, the Abrahams, who were already on route back to Memphis. Akbar Abraham was a well-known heart surgeon and his wife, Sophie, was a doctor as well. We knew that they would be able to explain to us what was happening with Abba.

Dr. Abraham called and spoke with Abba's doctor, then briefed Amma and us in Bengali. Later that evening after the Abrahams returned to Memphis, they insisted that we stay with them while Abba was in the hospital. It was convenient, especially since we didn't have a car, and they could drive us to and from the hospital. The few families that were living in Memphis at that time came to our help as well. People drove us to school, made us meals, and sometimes just sat with us and prayed. The doctor suggested that Abba needed open heart surgery in order to relieve the blood clot to his heart.

Dr. Abraham scrubbed into the surgery but only as an observer. Some six hours later, he came out and told us that there were some complications. Apparently, during the surgery, Abba suffered a stroke. Dr. Abraham pulled out a piece of paper and drew a heart and valves in order to explain what was happening with Abba.

The following day, we were able to visit him. Abba came in and out of consciousness. He told me to not worry, all would be fine.

But I was scared of the machines that were attached to him and always kept my distance. Abba called me to come closer to him, so hesitantly I did. I couldn't stop tears from running down my face.

With a quivering voice, I said, "Ami tomaya bhalobasi."

As soon as I said, "I love you," in Bengali to Abba, Amma pinched me. She didn't want me to upset Abba by saying such a thing.

Abba was in the hospital on my fifteenth birthday. I wore my ski jacket, even though the weather was in the 50s, and I went to school. After school, I went to the hospital to model my jacket for Abba. But he didn't recognize me. He was singing Debbie Boone's "You Light Up My Life" with his nurse.

His nurse finally stopped singing and said, "Your daughter is here. Today is her birthday," but Abba continued.

"You give me hope to carry on."

The nurse looked at me and said, "Your father is under a lot of medication. I am sure that it is all the drugs."

But he remembers the lyrics to the song, I thought to myself.

Those were my father's last words, "You light up my life; you give me hope to carry on. You light up my days and fill my nights with song." Later that day, Abba suffered a major stroke and was put on a ventilator.

It was the middle of the night when I was woken up and was told that the doctors wanted us at the hospital. I walked into the bathroom to put on my favorite blue top with embroidered daisies all over and my Calvin Klein jeans. I quickly put my hair in a ponytail and ran downstairs. We all loaded into the Abrahams' cars and headed to the hospital.

No one spoke in the car; only prayed. As we got off the elevator and started to make our way to Abba's room, I could see a group of men in white coats standing in front of Abba's room. His door was shut. The doctors asked us to sit down, and so we did.

He looked at Amma and said, "I am so sorry, but your husband suffered another stroke, and this time we couldn't save him."

I didn't understand what he was trying to tell us.

"We couldn't save him."

What does that mean, my friends? I asked. My

imaginary friends never left my side even though I relied on them less and less after our move to the States.

The doctors got up and opened Abba's door. The Abrahams were consoling Amma. My sisters were crying as I walked into his room. Abba looked like he was asleep. All the machines were gone as if they never existed. Abba laid on his hospital bed with eyes closed and a white sheet covering his entire body except for his face. He looked so peaceful that I didn't want to wake him. I could feel my friends' arms around me.

"He is just sleeping, right?" I asked, but no one said a word, nothing, as tears ran down their faces.

At sunrise, the Abrahams drove us to our apartment to get some clothes for Abba's funeral. My sisters and I took a traditional Bengali outfit that Amma had made for us several years back for an Islamic holiday. Long, white pants called sallower, and long, white tops called kameez with tiny silver polka dots all over. In traditional Islamic culture, people wear white to funerals, representing peace.

We had no relatives in Memphis, so all the Muslim family friends had pitched in to help with Abba's funeral expenses. My eldest sister was a senior in high school, middle sister in eleventh grade, and I was in the ninth grade. We had never attended a funeral and had no idea what to do. Also there were a lot of Islamic traditions that needed to be followed, so the elders took charge.

Islamic tradition requires that an individual is buried as soon as possible. Therefore, there wasn't enough time for any of our relatives to come down from Dhaka for the funeral. So we proceeded as quickly as possible. Finding a place to bury Abba was difficult. There wasn't any place within Memphis city limits that allowed us to observe Islamic burial traditions, so we decided to bury Abba at a small town called Munford. It was forty miles outside of Memphis.

Everything happened at warp speed. I had no time to process or grieve; there simply wasn't enough time. Amid the chaos, I started my period. Growing up in a Muslim home, I always knew that having your period meant you were considered dirty.

During a woman's menstrual cycle, she doesn't perform Namaz. I knew that there were taboos associated with a menstruating woman at burials. I wanted no harm for Abba and decided to tell my mother and others about my period.

I pulled Amma aside and whispered, "Amma, I started my period."

She looked angry and disappointed. I felt ashamed and guilty. It wasn't long before I became excluded from all burial and funeral plans. I wasn't allowed to touch anything because it would be "unclean."

People from all over came to Abba's funeral; most of them I didn't even know. All the cars lined up, and a long procession to Munford Funeral Home began. In the car, I leaned my head on my imaginary friends' shoulders as they handed me a beautiful bouquet of daisies, like the ones they gave me while in Dinajpur. We said nothing to each other as we gazed out the window. We had traveled far from the streets of Dinajpur together, but some things within us hadn't changed. I found comfort in their embrace as we looked at the road ahead.

People walked into the funeral home and took off their shoes. Everyone grabbed an individually bound set of papers, a chapter, from a pile. A total of thirty chapters completed the entire Koran, so the Islamic goal was to finish an entire Koran at least once collectively. I had learned how to read Arabic at our local mosque, but I was not allowed to read the Koran because of my period at Abba's funeral. I sat in the back alone and signaled my imaginary friends to join me, even though the men sat separately from the women. My friends were always very good at hiding.

A wooden box was rolled out and inside laid Abba. He looked different. He had been shaved and had cotton balls inside his nose. I had never seen anyone right before burial and had no idea what was done to the body. I stared at him with one question in my mind, *Can someone check to make sure that he is really dead?* But I didn't ask my question, only watched them take him away.

I wasn't allowed at the burial. All the women just remained behind at the funeral home while the men took Abba.

Most of the people there were our Muslim friends. Only a handful of American Christian friends attended Abba's funeral, perhaps due to the distance and not knowing our traditions. My school friend Samantha and her dad, Dr. Steven, came to Abba's funeral. Often Sam helped me with my studies, and I had had countless dinners at her home. I was envious of Sam's family and home. Sam's mom was a teacher, and her father listened to people's problems.

Dr. Steven did not join the other men at my father's burial, instead he sat with me outside.

"How can God punish Abba for having three daughters? There isn't a single family member at his burial? How is that fair?" I asked.

Dr. Steven nodded his head in agreement. Then he looked at me and said, "Why don't you research these questions? I bet you can find the answers to your questions." He continued, "I don't know Islam, but your questions are valid." Before leaving, Dr. Steven gave me his business card and said, "If you ever want to talk, I will be here for you. My door will always be open for you."

The loss of my father was devastating for me. He was my hero and role model. Since Amma barely left the house or spoke English, she had no way of supporting our family. Our relatives offered us to return to Bangladesh. The idea of a single woman living alone in America didn't seem reasonable to our relatives. Everyone worried about how we would support ourselves. Was it safe for four women to live without a man in the house?

I recall that my relatives suggested that my male cousin, who was only a year older than me, should come to live with us. And the idea of moving back to Bangladesh came up several times. We had countless long discussions and arguments regarding what to do. I knew that returning would mean arranged marriage and the end of my education. So my sisters and I agreed that we would get jobs and support ourselves.

While Abba was alive, he kept asking Nani to come visit. But Nani told him that such long travel would be too much of a hardship on her. She also didn't feel comfortable flying alone, especially since she didn't speak English. But after hearing of Abba's passing, Nani made the journey from Dhaka to Memphis in late 1982. I recall that she and I walked to a nearby ice cream shop, just the two of us, and I treated her. Amma had saved some beef in the freezer that Abba purchased and cooked it for Nani.

Nani and me at our apartment on South Morrison

Living with Amma became even more impossible after Abba's death. She had reverted back to her rants, frantic breathing, and pacing. Amma possessed the ability to stop her rants, her outbursts, every time someone knocked on the door. In presence of others, she acted fine and was an exceptional host. But as soon as they left, Amma would return to rants.

Every morning began worse than the last. At times, she kept my sisters and me up all hours of the night with her screams and panting. She woke up or perhaps never slept, early, very early. I heard her muttering to herself like she did in Dinajpur. She uttered words, phrases, senselessly, as if she had no control.

She screamed, "You are a sinner. You are a whore."

"Sinner, sinner," she screamed.

Her words pounded us as we desperately tried to get ready for school. We just wanted to leave the house as quickly as possible.

"You are worthless. No one will ever marry you... sinner, sinner." She got louder with each breath.

Amma told me that I should not decline any marriage proposals.

"Your abba's name will bring just so many proposals. You are not that great. You better think about accepting one of these marriage proposals if you know what is good for you."

A YEAR after my father's death, we were approved to take the citizenship test. My father had died while waiting to become an American citizen with his entire family.

During the naturalization ceremony, we were greeted by strangers waving the American flag and saying, "Welcome home."

I regret that my father did not experience the warm welcome that we received that day. Though he did not live to become an American citizen, he was patriotic.

According to Amma, our American citizenship was the only real leverage we had to "getting a man." I no longer had long hair, and I talked back too often to be an obedient wife to a Bengali man.

In her view, my future was bleak at best. Arranged marriage was my only hope.

Proposals began to arrive. Some were just phone calls to Amma from a third-party friend. They discussed the prospective husband's education, profession, and family history. We were not involved in the discussion.

Soon resumes with pictures arrived in our mailbox. Amma stuffed our picture in an envelope, entered it on the bride market. These men were not interested in us. They didn't even know us, but they were desperate to attain a green card through our American citizenship.

All of them looked revolting to me. I was not attracted to Bengali men, but it wasn't of any importance to Amma. She told me that I would have a secure future with a doctor for a husband. Happiness and love were secondary. Attraction was nonexistent. "You are not attractive," Amma said to me, as I laughed at the pictures and felt sorry for those guys.

I enjoyed watching rage consume Amma's face when I told her, "I don't believe in the institution of marriage."

Amma held the small life insurance money that Abba left us for wedding expenses. Every single dime that Abba left for our education was now directed toward getting the three of us married.

"If you want to go to college, you are on your own. No man wants to marry a woman more educated than him," Amma told me. I was determined to do the opposite of whatever Amma said. The more she tried to pull me away from school, the more determined I was to go to college.

Less than a year later, my eldest sister accepted a marriage proposal from a Bangla Muslim named, Akbor. I really didn't want Aisha to get married. I didn't want to be left alone with Amma again. Akbor insisted that they buy a big house, so my other sister, mother, and I could all move in with them.

Though it was a generous offer, it was a horrible idea. Akbor had no idea about Amma's rants. So Shati and I decided that we would move to a better apartment complex, something more centrally located, and not move in with Akbor and Aisha.

It was in my sophomore year of high school when we moved to an apartment complex near both our schools. It was a two-bedroom apartment with a large bathroom, a living area, a separate dining area, and a kitchen. We purchased a new cream color sofa set. It was our first new furniture purchase in America. Previously, all we owned were hand-me-downs.

Shati and I took the master bedroom with an adjoining bathroom. She and I divided the wall space, so we could hang posters. My side of the wall was full of magazine clippings of Michael Jackson, Duran Duran, and Erik Estrada. Amma took the second bedroom. Aisha's wedding plans were underway. Relatives from Bangladesh started to arrive after Aisha got engaged. It was the most joyous occasion in our family since our move to America. Relatives came in from Bangladesh, and Amma cooked up a storm.

I loved Akbor. He was a tender soul and showed genuine concern for me and our family. We created a bond rather quickly. He helped me build an elevator once for my school science project. He and I also attended a French play with my French class. And Akbor taught me to drive!

I felt safe confiding in him. So, one day, I told Akbor that I hadn't been to Abba's gravesite and how much I missed him. Akbor consulted his father about taking a female to a gravesite. He along with other Muslims believed that it was un-Islamic for women to visit the cemetery. I'd heard stories that a woman's presence at a gravesite can disturb peace, and women would be a distraction for any men praying at the gravesite. I had no intention of disturbing anyone; I just wanted to be close to my dad.

Akbor and his father agreed to take me. I wore traditional Islamic attire and covered my hair. The drive to Munford felt long, almost an hour. First, we drove by the funeral home; then slowly we made our way to the cemetery. A barbed wire fence surrounded row after row of tombstones. A sea of crosses and flowers filled the place. I sat up tall in hopes of spotting Abba's grave, but from the car, it was difficult for me to see. Akbor parked; then he and his father got out and walked to Abba's grave. I wasn't allowed to get out of the car. They pointed to a small tombstone, where Abba was buried. I prayed even though I no longer believed in God or Islam. After they finished praying, Akbor drove his car close enough for me to see Abba's tombstone. Somehow, seeing Abba's name written made his absence even more real and the feeling of utter loneliness consumed me. I cried the entire ride back home.

Amma's outbursts were not only loud, but she also constantly criticized us.

She started in the middle of the night, screaming, "Allah, Allah," loud enough to wake us up.

Then she paced the hallway chanting and saying things, like, "Murderer, killer."

I don't know if she was referring to herself or was calling us those names. Sometimes, I would get so mad that I couldn't fall back asleep. She seemed to not care if we had a test the following day. Her hurtful words and constant criticisms stripped me of any self-esteem that I had left.

The woman whom she portrayed in front of others, a loving widow left in a foreign country with three daughters, was not the woman I knew. Amma got a lot of attention and sympathy from others, but she never displayed any sympathy or compassion to her daughters. My sisters and I worked all hours of the day, doing grocery shopping, washing clothes at the Laundromat, everything that Abba did. Amma didn't care that we were grieving the loss of our father. She never took an interest in my schooling and never asked to see my report cards.

School was my source of escape from Amma and our home life. There were many mornings when I got up and threw on some clothes and went to school very early. The school janitor was nice and let me inside. I washed my face, brushed my teeth at the school bathroom. Often, my friend Samantha bought breakfast from her home, and we sat in the hallways and ate. I also changed my outfits at school. I was not allowed to wear mini-skirts or makeup. So I kept them in my school locker, and every morning, I put on makeup and changed my pants to skirts.

To contribute to the household expenses, I took a part-time job. A shop called China Town was walking distance from our apartment, and even though I wasn't legally old enough to work, Mr. Chang hired me. He gave me $2.50 an hour. I worked every day after school until 8 p.m. and both Saturdays and Sundays. I brought home $75.00 a week.

At China Town, I stocked shelves and priced items, and when it was slow, I did their laundry and ironed. Mr. Chang and his wife lived at the back of the store with their son. I envied their son, who came home from school and just sat and watched T.V. and ate snacks. Sometimes, he went outside and played with other kids. I rarely played with my friends. I was either at school, doing homework, or working.

Eventually, I got promoted to sales when Mr. Chang noticed that I communicated better with the customers. Twisted beads were the fad in the early 80s, and I sold various colors and created a wide variety of necklaces that women my mother's age loved.

It wasn't long before Mr. Chang asked me to come to work dressed nicely. "You, no more wash my clothes. You sell." And I gladly accepted my new role.

I enjoyed talking with customers and selling. I got so good at selling that he eventually raised my hourly wage to $4.

Writing in my diary, I found a business card that my friend Samantha's dad had given to me at Abba's funeral. It was several years ago that Dr. Steven had asked me to call whenever I needed anything. Steven's card read that he was a psychotherapist.

After days of agonizing, I dialed his number.

"This is Steven."

I held the phone in fear. I didn't know why I had called him anymore. "I am sorry; I should not have called...I am sorry."

Before I could hang up, he said, "Well, since you did call, why not tell me how you are doing?" He continued. "I know that accent and that apologetic voice anywhere. So, how are you?"

"I want to go to college, not just any college, but far away from Memphis."

"How are your grades?"

"I have straight As, and I am president of the Honor Society. Ms. Hills says that I can go anywhere but—" I paused.

"And your mother doesn't approve? I am free tomorrow afternoon; can you come to my office?"

"My mother has all of my money; I can't pay you. If I file for insurance, she'll know that I am seeing a shrink which would mean no marriage proposals."

I barely gasped for air before continuing, "Who wants to marry a crazy woman? I am sorry that I bothered you. I should not have called. Thank you, Dr. Steven."

"Tomorrow at 4 p.m., I will be waiting for you at my office."

I never made it past Steven's waiting room. Steven's waiting room was dark and cozy with two comfy couches with dimmed lights and stacks of books everywhere. A picture of Steven when he was much younger and had hair sat on a shelf along with a couple of art projects that Sam made when she was younger. Soft music played in the background as I sat on the couch and cuddled myself with a fluffy blue pillow. I could easily fall asleep there snuggled with a blanket. It felt so peaceful and safe.

Steven opened the door to his office and smiled a bit, as if he had been waiting for me all day and said, "Shama, come in." I didn't, couldn't move.

He stood for a minute, then smiled again, and said, "Let me join you."

Even though I had had dinner at his home numerous times, I felt nervous. He wasn't Sam's dad, not here. Perhaps he sensed my fear because that afternoon Steven stayed in his office with the door wide open, his chair facing me while I remained sitting on the couch in his waiting room. At our first meeting, he pulled his chair close but remained in his office. At our second meeting, he asked if he could move his chair closer to the door, so he could hear better and made jokes about his age. I liked his sense of humor.

At our fourth meeting, Steven and I sat in the waiting room together. The waiting room is where we talked for the next three months. He read my college entrance essays, helped me fill out college applications, and we talked about my childhood. I never told him about my sexual abuse, only that I needed to leave Memphis and get away from Amma. Steven always reminded me that he was safe; and he had no plans to go anywhere. I wanted to believe him even though I knew he too one day would leave me. I continued to remind myself to not be fooled by his temporary kindness. I couldn't trust anyone.

College acceptance letters along with marriage proposals filled our mailbox. I knew that I was safe until my older two sisters were married off. Amma wouldn't break our cultural tradition and let her younger daughter marry first. So, I kept hoping to leave Memphis upon graduation.

I had one goal, and that was to leave Memphis. I wanted to get as far away from Amma as possible; but more importantly, I did not want to have an arranged marriage.

I went to countless college fairs, read books on colleges, and applied. I was envious of my friends, Samantha and Charlotte, whose parents took such great interest in their college searches.

I remember receiving my first college acceptance letter from the University of Michigan. I was ecstatic. I rushed to Dr. Steven's office to find that he was in a session. So, I anxiously waited in the waiting room for his session to end. As soon as his client walked out the door, I ran in and gave him a big hug. He almost stumbled down to his seat.

"Dr. Steven, I got in," the words rushed out of my mouth.

He smiled big and said, "Lucky for them."

I don't know if I told him what college, and it didn't matter. I was finally leaving Amma.

When I returned home and told Amma that I was accepted to Michigan State, she was furious and straight out said, no.

"You are not going so far and to a college full of men," Amma declared.

I called Dr. Steven, crying. "Amma said no to colleges with boys." A sense of hopelessness filled my heart. "What do I do, Dr. Steven?" There was a silence.

"Help me," I said with absolute desperation.

Dr. Steven said, "Shama, there are women's colleges. We can apply to all-woman colleges."

He said "we" and that is all I needed to hear and feel at that moment.

The following day, I met with Dr. Steven, and he had a list of women's colleges all over the United States. I submitted my application to Wesleyan, Spelman, and Agnes Scott College. Less than a week later, I received a call from Agnes Scott College in Atlanta. They invited me to tour the campus. Amma reluctantly agreed.

My senior picture

I bought a pink shirt and blue floral silk blouse and some white flats to wear for my interview. An ASC representative met me at the airport and drove me to campus. Beautiful buildings surrounded by young women walking with backpacks and books, I wanted to start that very day. Everyone I met was extremely nice and welcoming. I had decided at that moment that, if I were offered a scholarship, I would accept.

In May of 1986, I graduated from Central High and prepared to leave Memphis to attend Agnes Scott College. Amma was in disbelief that I would go.

She told those who asked me about my college plans, "Let her think what she wants."

But with every roll of her eyes and comment of disbelief, I became even more determined to prove her wrong.

My sisters, Akbor, and I decided that we would take an extra few days and drive to Atlanta for a vacation. Afterwards, they would drop me off at ASC. On the morning of our trip to Atlanta, Amma started her rants. Screaming from the top of her lungs, saying that I was making a mistake.

Shati kept saying, "Shut up, Amma. Today is Shama's last day at home."

But Amma wouldn't stop. I opened my sister's suitcase and took out all of Amma's clothes and threw them out. I was determined to not let her ruin this moment for me. For once, I wanted Amma to not make it about her. But she was not capable.

I loaded my suitcase in my brother-in-law's car as Amma yelled from the balcony, "You are nobody; you will be back; you are making a mistake," and the car pulled away.

I wanted him to drive, just drive without stopping. I wanted to break free and never look back. "Faster, faster, I want to be in Atlanta. God, please help Akbor to go faster," I repeated. The fear of something happening that delayed or even prevented us from leaving frightened me. Just like I didn't want to go back to Golam's place that stormy day, I didn't want to go back to Amma. I just wanted to get to Atlanta. I wanted to escape.

That was the last time I lived in Memphis. I never looked back knowing that what lie ahead had to be far better. I left Memphis with the same sense of desperation that I had arrived on that cold March night. I left Memphis knowing that it was just another obstacle. It was not my destination. My American dream still waited.

6. Breaking Free

My sisters and I had fun in Atlanta despite Amma. And when the time came for my sisters to leave, they dropped me off at ASC. We all cried. I cried out of fear of the unknown, and perhaps, they cried knowing that I would never live with them again.

As they drove off, it reminded me of the times I stood on the windowsill at Nani's house, crying and waving goodbye. I used to hate watching the two of them leave with Boro Khala. I didn't want to be alone. To this day, my two sisters live in the same city and see each other often while I live hundreds of miles away.

A few days after they left, I started college. I never lived with so many Westerners. My classmates, my roommate, all were so different. Most of them had boyfriends or were constantly talking about boys. I had no interest in dating or boys. I wanted nothing to do with them. One afternoon, several of us piled into a car and headed to a local grocery store when one of the girls said, "I need to get my birth control prescription filled."

I was horrified. I had never heard of anyone talking about sex and not someone who wasn't married. But as I hung out with them, the topic of sex came up often. Some details were descriptive. One evening, during my junior year of college, we were all sitting and watching the TV show *Moonlighting* when one of my friends described love-making very casually. They were teasing me and saying that I needed to date.

As they described how two people had sex, I realized that Golam and I had had sex. I couldn't breathe. I didn't know what to say. My friends would think that I was this disgusting person who had sex with a much older man. The floodgate, the gate that I had kept locked for so many years, blew open, and there was no stopping it. Not only did I have sex with Golam, but so did Amma. I remember seeing them together. I could not get the sound of Golam's breathing out of my head. The sound engulfed me to a point I rushed to the bathroom and vomited.

The next day, I made an appointment to speak with our college counselor. Ms. Margaret was a nice woman, but she didn't understand my cultural or religious upbringing. She made suggestions and gave advice that I found unhelpful.

Though we met once a week for the remainder of my time at ASC, I never confided in her. I never told her about Golam. I feared that ASC would expel me if they knew the truth about my past. They would view me as a horrible example for the other students. I told no one my secret—except now I felt that I had to keep it to protect myself.

Those years were a struggle for me both emotionally and financially. I worked at the college library but had difficulty affording books and other supplies. ASC is a private college, and most of the girls came from wealthy families. I had very little and often felt out of place. During my sophomore year, I got a used car and was able to get a job at a movie theater at nights to help with my expenses.

At college, I began to question all the things I grew up learning. I decided to do an independent study during my senior year. My topic was the role of women in Islam. I was busy learning not only what was being taught in the classroom but also about me. The things that I grew up thinking were facts started to fall apart. Soon, I realized that not all Hindus hated Muslims; not all Pakistanis hated Bengalis; and Jews were friendly people like everyone else.

My trips home to Memphis slowly decreased. I started doing internships and studies abroad, whatever opportunity I got to avoid going to Memphis. My shift in thinking and beliefs upset Amma greatly. She feared that my independent thinking would make me less desirable to Muslim men.

Amma made several arrangements for me to meet Bengali Muslim men. These men, all much older than me, would show up at our house for dinner while I was home from college. I wasn't very kind to any of them, but I justified my behavior by saying I would make even a worse wife, so I was doing them a favor. Though none of them interested me, I was mostly afraid of men, especially Bengali men.

I graduated from college without having a single boyfriend or kissing a man. Amma was anxious as ever to get me married off. I knew that if I weren't in school, the pressure to get married would be very high, so I started applying for graduate school.

My independent study at ASC sparked some interest in me about Islam. I recall Dr. Steven telling me to research why women were not allowed at prayer times and especially during funerals when they were menstruating. So, I would get a master's degree in Islam and then go to law school.

Before entering graduate school, I wanted to visit Dhaka. I had just enough money to buy one round-trip plane ticket, but I wasn't worried. I knew that once I arrived in Dhaka, I would have zero expenses. Everyone would make sure that I had a place to stay and lots to eat. However, I did want to take a few gifts for everyone, especially my young nieces and nephews.

I still remember watching my older cousins and others opening their suitcases after their trips back from overseas. With eyes wide open, I watched as they took out gifts one at a time. Patiently, I would wait for my gift.

That evening, I would take my gift to bed with me and cuddle it like a baby as I slept. If I received an outfit, it stayed on my bed, so I could wear it the following day. The gift didn't matter as much as the fact that it traveled such great distance. That item in my hand traveled a farther distance than I could ever imagine, just knowing that was the best gift ever.

As I packed my suitcases for Dhaka, I wondered if my relatives would recognize me. Of course, they had seen current pictures of me, but would they recognize me? I was no longer the ten-year-old who clutched her father's hands while walking into the plane. I was now twenty-two years old with a BA from an American college. Not only did I speak English fluently, but I knew how to read and write. I lived alone, drove a car, earned an income; but more importantly, I had gained a sense of independence. Then it occurred to me that I may not recognize them. What if I am not be able to overlook the past and held resentments toward them?

I told myself, "Go with a clean slate and forget the past," without realizing that the past is never forgotten or erased. It shapes and molds us. It is sketched in our souls. Memories of our past afford us with options on how to proceed in life. We can either repeat or refrain. I chose the ladder and boarded the plane.

The flight was exhausting at best. Thirty-plus hours later, I touched down at Dhaka International Airport. As I made my way through the crowd, the magnitude of which I had forgotten, I was greeted by one of my uncles. They had planned a time that allowed me to zip through customs check. A younger gentleman, who I later discovered was the driver, grabbed my suitcase and took the lead as my uncle and I followed. Making small talk, we approached his vehicle. A swarm of beggars engulfed me, making it impossible for me to move. My uncle yelled at them and the driver to move quickly.

"Shammu Mia," he said, referring to me. An affectionate variation of my name that Abba and others used in my younger days. "Can't believe you are here," he continued.

"I am so glad to be here," I said with some doubts.

We didn't engage in any long discussion on route to his house. The sounds from the traffic and constant honking of horns made it difficult to hear one's own thoughts, let alone someone else's. Once we arrived, the driver honked his horn, and everyone swarmed out of the house, as if someone poured hot water on an ant hill.

Taking a deep breath, I jumped out of the car. Hugs and kisses and hugs continued as they ushered me inside. My aunts and uncles yelled at the housekeepers to bring tea, paratha. "You must be starving?" someone asked.

But before I could answer, someone else suggested that I go and freshen up. Then another asked if I needed to sleep and inquired about my jet lag. I didn't take a nap but did freshen up and sat at the dining room table with tea.

For some reason, I expected to see the same young faces that waved goodbye to us back in 1978. But they all looked aged, making my heart ache knowing I may never see them again. Though I was jet lagged, I insisted on going to see Nani who due to poor health did not come to the airport.

Nani's hair had thinned, and so had she. Her once strong, forceful body was now fragile. I hugged her gently in fear of breaking her. Her eyes and teeth still danced and sparkled like before as she stared at me.

Nani had moved in with my youngest uncle when her health began to fail. My uncle insisted that he take over her care. During my trip to Dhaka, every day, I visited Nani but did not stay at my uncle's house. My elder cousin Kazi's house had Westernized amenities, so everyone insisted that I stay there for comfort.

Before leaving Dhaka, I went to Dhrobo Mama. I heard that he now occupied Nani's old flat with his wife and their daughter. Boro Khala's driver took me to Dhrobo Mama's flat for a visit. Nani's flat brought back memories of sitting on the corner of the bed with my book open. I had tried desperately to not mess up, as I read out loud, in order to avoid Dhrobo's paddle.

When I went inside, I saw Amma's glass display case with dolls that Abba bought from his overseas trip had not moved. I walked over and saw the Russian dolls, little geisha girl, Turkish doll—all displayed beautifully. The small bed where I slept was no longer there. Nani's bedroom was converted into a large living room for entertaining. Mama's wife and I spoke briefly. Our exchange felt awkward and forced. I made some excuse and told her that I couldn't stay long. Before leaving, I handed her a bag that included a couple of bottles of shampoo, lotion, toothpaste, and other toiletry items that were difficult to attain in Dhaka.

Several hours later, I received a call from Dhrobo Mama. His voice still intimidated me, though I tried my best to sound confident.

"Salam Mama," I said with a shaky voice. "Sorry I missed you earlier."

"I saw the things you dropped off. What you think that you are something special because you came from America? Do you think that we need your things?" he said with a familiar angry voice.

"That was not my intention. I," before I could finish, he continued, "We don't need your things. We don't need anyone's charity or pity."

After a few seconds of silence, I said, "Khuda hafit," meaning, *May Allah protect you*, and hung up the phone.

That was the last time we spoke, and the first time that I realized his anger had nothing to do with me. I simply served as his outlet, and now, he had no control over me. Nani overheard our conversation and attempted to make excuses for his behavior. Though I acted indifferent to his comments, that small child inside of me wept.

During that visit, Nani and I spent many hours together on her bed. I told her about college and plans for graduate school. I tried my best to update her with every big and small detail of my life in America. But not once did she or I mention Dinajpur or Golam. I knew that the past was not a welcomed topic of discussion.

On my final day in Dhaka, Nani asked my khala to bring her the sari. "The Sari" is a beautiful, purple silk garment with gold threading. It has been a part of our family for generations. The family tradition required that Nani's eldest son's wife inherited first, her second son's wife next, then her third son's wife, her eldest grandson's wife, and so on. However, that day, Nani gave me that sari and said, "Shamsuddin was like a son to me. I want you to have this."

I asked, "Are you sure?"

I knew that by taking the sari, I was not only breaking a family tradition, but taking the sari outside of Bangladesh into America. But once Nani made up her mind, there wasn't any going back. Upon returning to the States, I did receive a call from one of my uncles saying that it really should go down male lineage. And that Nani should not have broken the family tradition.

To which I replied, "It was Nani's to break."

I still have her sari in my possession. When my eldest daughter was a toddler, I had professional photographs taken of her with the sari and sent it to Nani. One day, my daughter will inherit it, as she is Nani's namesake.

A few years later, Nani passed away. I received the call while eating dinner with my family. It is strange to mourn the death of someone who is not a regular part of your life. Nothing was going to change in my life except I knew that the next time I visited Dhaka, nothing would be the same without Nani.

Nani wore a gold necklace along with a pendant with an inscription saying, *Bilmillah*, meaning "in the name of God." Upon her death, my uncle sent that necklace to my eldest daughter. At Miriam's eighteenth birthday, I gave her Nani's necklace.

I was twenty-three years old in graduate school with no marriage prospect in site. Proposals from Bangladesh had dwindled down to nothing. I was now too old, and Amma reminded me. I still hadn't dated or showed any interest in marriage. And apparently my childbearing years were numbered. Amma's frustration grew, and some questioned my sexual orientation due to my lack of interest in men. No one, especially family, asked about my hesitation of dating a man, and I did not share.

During graduate school, I lived in a studio apartment with no furniture, not even a bed. I worked the graveyard shift at Montgomery Wards and went to class during the day. The only life I knew was studying and working. I didn't socialize; I barely had time for sleep. At graduate school, I became a vegetarian, partly because I didn't like the idea of eating animals and partly because I couldn't afford to buy meat.

At graduate school in Tallahassee, I decided to write my thesis on the perception of blood in Islam. This topic required me to research and study various cultural norms that were intertwined with religious teachings, some Islamic but mostly Hinduism. Many people accepted these traditions, such as a woman who was menstruating not being able to attend a burial, as part of Islamic practice, without understanding the cultural influence. I will say that many Islamic scholars disagree with my findings, but I hold firm in my beliefs. And given the same circumstances today, I would attend my father's burial.

During my last semester, I met Jonathan. He was a Texan studying Eastern religions. Jonathan was very interested in Eastern culture. We spent a lot of time going to the beach with a bunch of other grad students in our department, and we had numerous study groups together. I felt comfortable and safe with him. I didn't really see him as a love interest and was certain that he liked my friend Carrie. One Saturday, on our way back from the beach, Jonathan, Carrie, and I sat in the backseat and talked the entire four-plus hours drive.

Jonathan was the first drop-off, and as he got out of the car, he leaned in and asked, "Want to come over to my place later to study?"

I was certain that he was talking to Carrie, but she insisted that he was talking to me. To test her theory, Carrie called Jonathon and said that she couldn't make it and hung up the phone, A few minutes later, Jonathan called me to say that Carrie couldn't make it, but he was hoping that I was still coming. I was a little surprised but told myself that he just needed my help with his upcoming exam on Hinduism.

That evening, I walked up to his apartment, carrying my book and notes, and rang the doorbell. He opened the door with a big smile. His apartment was small but cozy. Several guitars, both electric and acoustic, were placed in almost every corner of the room. With incense burning and tabla (Indian instrument) playing in the background, it was dreamy. I thought to myself that he had remembered I played the tabla.

Jonathan offered me a place to sit and some tea. His small kitchen was separated by a wood divider, just enough to create an impression that it was a different room. We sat down on his futon couch, me still holding my book. However, that evening, either one of us opened our books. Instead, we sipped tea, listened to Indian acoustic, and talked about Buddhist teachings. I was in an awe by his depth of knowledge and insight. I had never met a man with so much intelligence.

As I got up to leave for the evening, he reached over to give me a hug. I froze. The only man I hugged was Abba, and I did not know how to respond to Jonathan's gesture. He retreated quickly, and we both awkwardly said goodbye. On the drive back to my apartment, I felt something that I had never experienced. I had butterflies and a grin on my face that lasted for days.

The following day after class, he asked me out on a date. This time, he offered to come over and pick me up for dinner. Carrie came over to help me pick out an outfit. I was giddy with joy. He didn't try to hug or kiss me on our first official date. I did share with him that I had never dated and had some childhood trauma with abuse. We never discussed in detail about my past, but he was patient.

A few weeks into our dating, I celebrated my twenty-fifth birthday with him. That evening, I kissed him for the first time. I told him that Islam forbids premarital sex and that I wasn't willing to cross that line. There were times when both of us struggled with my decision to abstain, but we did not cross the line. Though our relationship struggled, we continued to date for over two years.

One evening over fondue dinner, he proposed, and I said yes. In retrospect, I was incapable of loving another person before I learned how to love myself. But I wanted to love and be loved. I desperately wanted to feel "normal." And getting engaged felt like the right next step in our relationship, especially since he was looking at a Ph.D. program in various states and the possibility of a long-distance relationship was apparent.

Amma and the rest of my family were ecstatic, despite the fact Jonathan was an American Christian. He was exactly the type of man Amma feared that I would marry if I attended co-ed colleges. But she was thrilled that at least I wasn't attracted to women. And to further sweeten the deal, I asked Jonathan if he would consider converting to Islam to which he said yes. We both didn't practice any faith, so as far as he was concerned, nothing would really change.

Once my family heard of Jonathan's decision to accept Islam, they hosted a big traditional engagement party. For once, Amma was happy with me. She never asked about our relationship or how Jonathan treated me. She was simply happy that the entire Islamic community in Memphis knew that my mother had successfully married off all three of her daughters.

Jonathan and I weren't in a hurry to get married. He began his Ph.D. in Austin, and I remained in Tallahassee due to work. We attempted a long-distance relationship but soon realized that it was not for us. In 1995, I moved to Austin to be with him. Amma started pressing us to set the wedding date. To please both of our families, we told them that we would marry after he received his Ph.D. Though that bought us time with our family, our relationship still struggled.

My mother began planning our wedding and making arrangements. Every time when someone went to Dhaka,

Amma gave them a list of items to purchase for my wedding. She was set on having a traditional Bangla wedding. I found myself caught in a position of pleasing either Jonathan or my family. My own happiness, wants, and desires were always secondary. I so desperately wanted to please Amma. I longed for her love, and marrying an American who converted in order to marry me, in my mind, was the ticket to Amma's love.

My move from Tallahassee to Austin was challenging. This time, I wasn't moving because of school. I didn't have a network of friends. So, I started looking for a job as quickly as possible.

At first, I went to various temp agencies, anything to keep me busy while Jonathan was in class. Eventually I got a job at a small law office doing secretarial and some paralegal work. And in the evenings, I was working retail at a local mall.

My long hours kept me away most of the time. Jonathan became completely consumed with his studies and his classmates, and we barely saw each other.

One evening Jonathan casually mentioned that he wasn't sure about getting married, not just after graduation but ever. At this point, I didn't even know if I wanted to marry him either, but I did not want to bring more shame to my family. Everyone in Memphis who attended our engagement party would now know that we broke up, I thought to myself.

So, I kept delaying telling my family, but the longer I waited, more they proceeded with the wedding plans. In the meantime, I kept looking for a better job and was finally able to secure a job with a nice law firm.

One afternoon Jonathan came home early from classes and told me that he wanted to move out. Though I knew that it was the best decision for the both of us, I did not know how to tell my family. I felt ashamed and humiliated to a point that I began to isolate myself. Our breakup also stirred up many unresolved issues of abandonment and childhood abuse. I fell deep into a depression. As I think back, the humiliation of having to tell my mother the news felt more painful than our breakup. *Perhaps she was right, I am a throwaway*, I thought to myself countless times.

My life consisted of going to work and counting the hours until I returned to work. The only company I had outside of work were my cats. Throughout my life, I had contemplated suicide. I always viewed suicide as an option, a way to take control of my situation. I wanted to end my life in Dhaka when my uncle pounded me and when the pain of not seeing my family overwhelmed me with grief and after Abba's death.

But this time, the thought of suicide consumed me every day. I felt both physically and mentally exhausted and wanted out. However even with my struggle with depression, I managed to function every day. I went to work on time, paid my bills on time, took care of my cats —I functioned like a "normal" person.

I celebrated my birthday alone in my apartment. And the following day, I began to make plans to end my life. I wanted to make certain that whatever means I used, it had to work. The fear of being brain dead or paralyzed and needing my mother to take care of me was far greater than any sadness I felt.

Having to constantly pretend to be someone else was exhausting. I felt shame every time Amma told me about my younger cousin's wedding. My college friends were giving birth, and I was completely alone with no friends. One day after work, I went over to my neighbor Bryan and gave him a piece of paper with my sister's address and asked him to promise me that if something ever happened to me that he would take my cats to Memphis. Bryan was confused but promised.

The following evening, I drove to six different drug stores and bought a bottle of sleeping pills from each. I did not know how many pills I needed and wanted to make certain that I had enough. I came back to my studio apartment and emptied all the bottles into a salad bowl.

I took a bottle of wine out of the refrigerator and stood in front of my bathroom mirror. I hated the girl looking back at me. She was weak. She was unwanted. She was a throwaway, except no one had courage to throw me away. I had to do it. My hand scooped fist full after fist full of pills as I swallowed them down with wine. There was a moment when I contemplated calling Amma. I wanted to tell her that I knew that Golam had sex with me; I knew that she cheated on Abba.

Amma, I remember it all, I wanted to tell her. I wanted her to feel my despair. I wanted her to hurt. I wanted her to feel the pain of my flesh ripping apart each time Golam went inside of me. But everything was blurry. I couldn't dial the phone. I just stumbled around my apartment until I passed out.

I had given Bryan keys to my apartment, so he could feed my cats when I worked late or traveled. That evening, he happened to let himself in my apartment thinking that I wasn't at home, so he could feed my cats. Instead, he found me on my bathroom floor unconscious. He carried me down the stairs to his pickup truck and rushed me to the hospital. I remember fading in and out and shivering. Bryan had all the windows rolled down and the radio blaring. He tried to keep me from falling asleep as he sped to the hospital.

At the hospital, the doctors and nurses all hovered over me. They held my neck down and forced me to drink charcoal. I tried to fight and begged them to let me die. But they kept forcing me to drink. The charcoal ran down the side of my face, and I gagged and gasped for air. I faded in and out of consciousness each time hoping that I would not wake up, but I did. They asked Bryan to rush to my apartment and bring back all the empty bottles.

Before leaving for my place, Bryan called Jonathan to tell him. I don't have full memory of that night. I do remember that the nurse kept asking me if there was someone that they could call. I told her that I had no one. I was too old to believe in imaginary friends, and Abba was dead. And I didn't want them to call my family.

I was put under a twenty-four-hour watch. My arms were strapped down. If I needed to use the toilet, someone sat with me. A psychiatrist came to see me several times. He asked me to rate my feelings on a scale of one to ten.

"Where is your mood?" he asked me.

"I want to die," I replied, annoyed.

They asked questions that if one wanted to get out of the hospital, they knew the obvious answers.

It didn't take very long for the charcoal to take effect. Slowly, my vision became clearer, and I became more aware of my surroundings, when I noticed Jonathan near my bed. He looked utterly mad at me, as if my suicide attempt were to punish him.

I recall asking him to kiss me.

He looked at me and said, "You look terrible, Shama. You have charcoal all over you."

Then he stopped and asked with shame in his voice, "You know that you are in the psych ward?"

I said nothing but looked away. That was the last time that I saw or spoke with Jonathan.

My family had no idea that I was in the hospital, only Bryan and Jonathan knew. After five days of hospital stay, I was released. Bryan took care of my cats while I was in the hospital. After I returned to my apartment, Bryan told me that an attorney from work came looking for me. He said that he covered for me and told him that I had a death in the family and went to Memphis.

After a couple of days, I returned to work. I didn't know what I would tell them about not showing up to work, but before I could say anything, they called me into the conference room. I was certain that I was about to get fired.

The lead attorney looked at me and said, "We have decided to make an investment. We decided to invest in you."

Apparently, Bryan had a change of heart and told them about my suicide attempt. The attorney said, "We will pay your hospital bill, and we have found you a therapist. We will pay for all your sessions and whatever medication you may need. You are not alone, Shama."

That was the first time anyone ever said those words to me.

He then handed me a card and said, "Charles is waiting for your call."

I called and made my first appointment with Charles. And my boss handed me a typed-up check already made out to Charles for his fees.

I arrived at his building and sat in the parking lot, trying to sum up the courage to walk in. Charles's office building faced Lake Austin. The view was breathtaking. I walked around, stalling. Then finally, I knocked on his door.

Charles was a tall man with short, grayish hair. He was a handsome man with an unshaved face, like he was in a hurry getting dressed that morning. He wore jeans and a t-shirt. There was something gentle about the way he smiled. He greeted me and said that he had heard a lot about me.

"You are loved and appreciated by many from what I hear," he said as he directed me to sit.

The couch was cream color with rusty orange pillows with ties on each end. The couch faced Lake Austin, though Charles sat directly in front of me. There stood a serenity fountain next to his desk and a bookshelf filled with books on Zionism and Buddhism.

Reluctantly, I sat down. I was nervous beyond words. I really didn't want to see a therapist, but I didn't want to disappoint my boss. Charles felt like another person who I needed to pretend for. I needed to perform, so he could tell my boss that I no longer needed therapy. That I was cured. I was tired of pretending. I was tired of performing. So I decided that I would go to my sessions with him but would not speak.

I simply walked into my session with a book in hand. I sat down and before Charles could say hello, I looked down at my book and started reading. This went on for several sessions when finally, Charles had enough.

"Let me explain how therapy works. We have a conversation."

I looked up and rolled my eyes, took out his check and put it on the coffee table, and continued to read.

At every session, Charles would ask questions to which I did not reply. Sometimes, he told me about something that his dog did that morning, and I would reply, "Not interested."

Charles once asked me if I could help him find more clients like me, "This is sweet. I just sit here and watch you read and get paid. I need more clients like you."

To which I replied, "Asshole."

After our session, I returned to the office, and if my boss asked about my session, I told him that it was going great. Five weeks went by when one day, I came into Charles's office to find him lying on his couch reading a book. Charles didn't even look up to say hello. I made some loud gestures, hoping to get his attention, but he was deep into his book. I was annoyed. *I am paying this guy to listen to me*, I thought to myself. So, I took my book and threw it at him.

Charles sat up and said, "Let me tell you about the book I'm reading."

He told me about *A Map of the World* by Jane Hamilton. We talked about grief and utter sadness. Charles gave me a copy of that book which I still have. At first, we talked about my daily routine. I showed him pictures of my sisters and of Abba.

I started seeing him three times a week, and we spoke every day including weekends. It was as if I had stored so much inside of me that there wasn't enough time in the day to tell him all. We went on walks near his office. We talked about my imaginary friends and the flowers we picked in the field of Dinajpur.

Charles often gave me homework. Once he gave me a tape recorder and asked me to stand in front of my mirror and say whatever came to mind.

"You are such a reject. I hate you. You couldn't even kill yourself. You can't do anything right," I screamed looking at myself in the mirror. It was the same mirror that watched me swallow six bottles of sleeping pills. The following session, he hit play, and we both listened. I cried and began to tell him about Golam and my uncle. I told him about barrel and the canopy bed. I told him my secret.

We spent many sessions talking about Amma. One day, I walked into our session and said, "Charles, I want to confront my mother and ask her why she let Golam do those things to me. I want her to know that I remember."

Charles sat back, and though he never came out and told me what to do before, he said, "I just don't think that it is a good idea."

I was surprised by his response. He then continued, "I fear that your mother will not give the answers that you are looking for. She will leave you feeling abandoned again."

"But Charles, I want her to know that I know her secret."

Charles replied, "When you are stronger, maybe then. But for now, it is important that we keep you from harmful, poisonous people."

I didn't take Charles's advice. I went to Memphis and told my sister that I needed to ask Amma questions about Dinajpur. I told her that my therapist suggested that I speak with Amma. That afternoon in my sister's backyard, Amma and I sat down to talk privately. "I want to talk about Dinajpur, Amma," I told her.

I could already sense her hesitation. I could already sense that she was annoyed by the topic. But I continued, "How could you let those things happen to me? Why didn't you protect me from Golam?"

Amma looked at me and replied, "I don't know what you are talking about."

"I know that you think I forgot. You think that I was too young to remember, but I remember it all, Amma," I replied angrily.

She didn't ask what I remembered. She only responded, "What do you want me to say, Shama? Do you want me to say that I am sorry? OK fine, I am sorry."

That was the last time that I ever talked about Dinajpur with Amma.

After, I returned to Austin and went to see Charles.

"How was your trip?" he asked.

I said nothing, and we sat in silence for almost the entire hour. I never cried in front of Charles, and I knew if I told him about the conversation with Amma, I would start crying. I learned early on to not cry. Golam and my uncle shamed me and beat me hard if I cried. But now that it was safe for me to show emotions, I didn't know how.

After an hour of trying to compose myself, I finally broke my silence and said, "You were right, Charles, she didn't apologize."

Charles replied, "Some things can't ever be forgiven."

I left his office, sat in my car, and cried.

———

AT THE START of every session, Charles always asked, "Shama, tell me something you know today that you didn't know yesterday."

Sometimes I told him some trivia that I learned about a foreign country or some other random thing, though I knew that he wanted me to tell him of some self-realization I had. Though I didn't willingly share my feelings, at his funeral, I read "The Guest House," a poem written by Rumi.

Charles was my guide from beyond. "The goal of a therapist is to get you to a place where you don't need them," he would say.

And as our work progressed, I saw him less frequently. Sometimes, I simply called and said, "Just checking in. I'll see you next week."

Charles never made me feel guilty for canceling. "Glad to hear! This means that you are doing your homework, kid."

And I did. I spent many evenings journaling and writing down every fragment of my memories from my childhood. I filled stacks and stacks of journals; and when I couldn't find the words to describe my feelings, I drew. I joined multiple support groups and surrounded myself with individuals who saw the best in me.

The following year in late fall, Liam moved into the apartment across from me. I invited him to a Bengali dinner at my place with other neighbors.

Liam replied, "I can't handle spicy food, but I will bring dessert."

That evening, he bought cheesecake and told of a place in Austin that served the best cheesecake ever. The following Saturday, he took me there to try it for myself.

Liam and I connected immediately. We both enjoyed museums and theater. Liam spoke softly unlike my family. I often found myself asking him to repeat because I couldn't hear.

I was attracted to his smile and didn't mind that he had thinning hair or that he wore a cross. He watched my cats when I traveled, and I looked after his place when he was out of town. He and I began to date. Amma was excited that finally I was interested in a man again, though his religious beliefs were a huge concern for her.

I told Charles that I went out with a guy and wasn't afraid.

He smiled big and said, "Baby steps."

We did take baby steps and dated for almost three years before Liam asked me to marry him. I was thirty-one years old. Liam and I didn't have a formal wedding. My family didn't approve of me marrying a Christian man, so to avoid any conflict, the two of us went to the justice of the peace in Austin. But I still wore a traditional Bengali outfit on my special day. I had my hair styled and makeup professionally done. Liam sent a limo to pick me up from my apartment. I met him at the front steps of the courthouse. We hired a photographer who took pictures at our civil ceremony with the judge who presided over our wedding. My wedding did not resemble any of my childhood fantasies. No one came from my or Liam's side of the family.

On our wedding night, what I thought would come so naturally for us, did not. It was an awkward encounter for both of us. I was terrified and could not relax. My mind and my body were not in-sync. Here, we were married and spending our first wedding night at a beautiful bed and breakfast, yet I could not relax.

Images of Golam on top of me haunted me, but I didn't tell Liam. He knew nothing about my abuse. He assumed that I didn't want to engage in sexual intercourse until we were married due to my religious and cultural upbringing.

The next day before leaving for our honeymoon, I called my doctor, and she prescribed a muscle relaxer for me. In Barcelona, after taking some muscle relaxer and drinking some wine, I made love for the first time. It took months before I no longer had to take drugs to relax. I did multiple relaxation exercises in order to eliminate Golam from my mind.

Both Liam and I wanted to start a family as quickly as possible. At thirty-three, I gave birth to our first daughter. We named her Miriam Nurjahan, meaning light of the world, after Nani. When I came home from the hospital, I called Nani and told her. She was beyond excited.

"All of you love me, but Shama always loves me more," she told everyone proudly.

I did love Nani and believed that she did her best to protect our family. Nani, with no formal education, in a male-dominated society, where religious restrictions compounded women's barriers, managed to remain in charge of her finances, estate, and her independence. Her intentions were well-meaning, though at times it felt like avoidance. As an adult, I understand that her perceived unwillingness, even blatant denial, were due to her limited internal and external resources. She simply did not know what to do and/or how to respond to my situation in Dinajpur.

With the news of my daughter's birth, Amma came down to Dallas and stayed with me for a week, though her original plan was to stay for a month.

I recall calling my sister and saying, "Either she flies off tomorrow, or she can wait at the airport for her flight next month."

Amma didn't know how to help. She only knew how to criticize. "Shama, you are holding her too tightly."

"Her diaper isn't on properly," she repeated.

When Miriam was a couple months old, I flew to Memphis to visit my family. I had always hoped that motherhood would create a bond between my mother and me. However, on that visit as I watched Amma pick up Miriam, I realized that I could never understand how she allowed others to abuse her own child. I realized that I am not her. I never want to be her. I did not require her approval, mostly because I didn't approve of her.

Three years later, I gave birth to my second daughter, Mira Eman. And our family was complete.

OUR ELDEST WAS BARELY six years old when I heard about Boro Khala's failing health. She had been on dialysis for several years, and it was taking its toll on her. After multiple discussions regarding leaving my girls behind, I decided to make the journey back to Bangladesh to see Boro Khala. I wanted to see her, and in retrospect, I was looking for some answers. Growing up, I always wondered why she didn't love me as much as my sisters. Why she didn't take me in like she did my two sisters. I knew that this was my last opportunity to ask, and no matter how painful it may be for me to hear, I wanted to know.

I woke up millions of miles away in a comfy bed at my cousin's house in Dhaka. The room was surprisingly quiet, especially since from the window I could see countless people, rickshaws, and traffic on the street below. My cousin had soundproofed windows installed that kept the sound of hustle and bustle of Dhaka at bay. But there was no escaping the view from the window. Tents made from old saris, someone cooking, vendors, all were just a couple of feet away.

I didn't sleep much. The time difference kept me up most of the night, though I took several melatonin the night before. I got dressed and went downstairs for breakfast. Afterwards, I went down another level to Boro Khala's room. Everyone always said that Khala was beautiful, though I never paid much attention to her physical appearance. I considered her beautiful for different reasons. I recall her being unbelievably kind and forgiving. And there were many times, I needed forgiveness.

Once my sister, cousin, and I were on the roof of her house and decided to tie a rope to my waist. The plan was that they would lower me down to the ground. Boro Khala had just happened to come out and nearly fainted.

"Get down from there" she yelled. "You guys are going to give me heart palpitations," she cried.

The three of us did come down, using stairs and not a rope, thinking that punishment was waiting for us.

But Boro Khala instead gave us a hug and said, "I would have been heartbroken if you guys got hurt."

I recall feeling ashamed that I caused her so much worry. In the absence of my own mother, I looked at Boro Khala as my own. Though she never asked and probably never even crossed her mind, I would have proudly called her Amma. And even after so many years and after giving birth to my own daughters, I still wanted to know why Boro Khala, like my mother, did not want me.

On the other side of the door, Boro Khala was laying on her bed with the television turned on. Next to her sat a remote, not for the TV, but for her to buzz for assistance. My cousin had set up his mother's room with every available modern convenience and technology to make her comfortable. The moment our eyes met, she said, "Are you afraid?" referring to her frail appearance. And I was not. I was sad.

My eyes watered, but I forced a smile and said, "Khala, it is so good to see you."

I sat on her bed, and we spoke about my girls. I showed her pictures, and she pointed out pictures all around her room. As I walked around and looked at the pictures, time stood still. Everyone looked so young, so full of dreams and ambitions. At that moment, I wanted to go back in time, except this time, I would have the courage to ask her to let me stay with her. This time, I would tell her that Dhrobo Mama abused me. I would tell her that I wanted to be with my sisters. I would tell her so much.

But all those questions that I left Dallas and my daughters behind to ask her suddenly felt selfish. This skeleton of a woman who showered me with love at every opportunity, I told myself, did not need to know my regrets. Instead, I simply laid next to her feeling happy that at that moment, she chose me.

I asked my youngest uncle to take me to visit Nani's grave. She had died several years earlier after suffering from Alzheimer's. Though I did not see her before she died, I had spoken with her often on the phone. She sounded fragile and incoherent. Her death did not come as a surprise; however, it was painful just the same. Nani was the only constant adult in my life growing up. Her passing was the start of an avalanche, as one by one each of my aunts and uncles began to pass away.

I had never been to a graveside in Dhaka. The only burial ground I'd ever visited was the cemetery in

America where Abba was buried. In Muslim cultures, women have strict dress rules, especially at burial grounds. To avoid any awkwardness, I'd inquired earlier on the suitable dress code for the venue. There were also varying views on women's presence at the graveside at all. Some Muslims believed that women should be forbidden to visit burial grounds all together.

Aware of the controversy, I played it safe and covered my legs and wore a long-sleeve shirt. I even borrowed a scarf from my cousin to cover my hair.

My uncle did not object to my request to visit Nani, which frankly was a surprise to me. Nonetheless, I was glad that he agreed to grant my wish. Due to the shortage of land, it was not uncommon to bury family members on top of one another, so Nani was buried in the same plot as my grandfather.

My uncle's driver wove in and out of traffic as my uncle and I sat in the back. I didn't know what to expect. Mama kept pointing to various landmarks, none of which looked familiar to me, and told me stories from my childhood. After what it felt like hours of driving, we made it to Nani's grave.

I was surprised to see vendors and crowds of people. I had expected the gravesite to be a quiet, solemn place, but it was not. Vendors sold bottled water, and young children asked for money from mourners, as if the city grew around the gravesite. My uncle rushed me through the crowds to a bricked rectangle wall covered with wildflowers. There were no tombstones at Nani or Nana's grave. Muslims don't believe in tombstones; grave marking is discouraged in

Islam. Monuments are viewed as idol worship to which Islam is opposed.

I stood there with my head-lowered, expecting to feel pain, anger, and grief. But I felt nothing except that I was twenty years too late. I wanted to ask Nani why she didn't rescue me from Golam sooner. I wanted to ask why she didn't protect me instead of asking me to keep secrets. But after only a few silent minutes, my uncle and I returned to the car. I felt relieved that I did my duty, but I had no closure.

Nani's gravesite stirred up mixed emotions for me. Growing up, Nani was my sole agent, my role model. I even named my elder daughter after her. I had never questioned her role in my abuse since she never hit me. However, Nani did not stop Golam or remove me from him. But then, I always felt an enormous amount of gratitude towards her. She had finally taken me into her home when no one else wanted me; why did that no longer feel like enough? Did her responsibility end with providing me shelter? I was asking questions now that I hadn't asked of her at seven years of age. A sense of betrayal consumed me for asking these questions of her and Boro Khala now. Though as an adult I can rationalize and even understand some of the logic behind both Nani and Khala's decisions, the child inside of me wanted confirmation that they did want me. And that their decisions, although they may have been faulty, were made with the utmost love for me.

I left Dhaka after only four days of stay. I needed to return home for my children. But I felt satisfied. In some strange way, I felt that by making a special trip to see

Boro Khala, I had done something for her. At the end, I had nothing but love to give her.

MY QUEST TO find answers and some peace within me continued, as I sought guidance from various therapists. But the biggest form of therapy came for me in writing and telling my story. In 2014, my essay on childhood sexual abuse and my suicide attempt was chosen for a local show titled, *Oral Fixation.* This show featured nine storytellers on stage, sharing our most vulnerable, personal details of our lives. The theme for this show was titled, "Elephant in the Room."

As I rehearsed for my presentation, the fear of being judged, being called a slut by the people in the audience, consumed me. It would be the first time that I openly shared my "secret" outside my therapist's office.

Like my abuse, my family never talked about my suicide attempt. I never told them how I tried to end my life, and they never asked. But now, I was about to share it all with strangers. At that time, I was working for a nonprofit helping to lead the efforts to raise awareness and funding for those suffering from mental illness and depression. I invited my boss and a couple of friends to attend and hear my story.

As the spotlight turned on me with "Brave" sung by Sara Bareilles, blaring in the background, I stood in front of a podium and began. In *Daring Greatly,* Dr. Brene Brown writes about shame. She states that shame gets its "power" from silence. So if we are able to speak about what's bringing us shame, we shed light on it and destroy it.

I was drowning in shame, but that evening I took the first step to exposing light on my shame. After the show, I was overwhelmed by the support, words of encouragement, and especially empathy that I received from total strangers.

The following morning at our management team meeting, my boss pulled me aside and said, "Thank you for inviting me."

Though my family never asked me to share the YouTube link of my presentation, I knew that it was out there and the secret was no longer mine to keep.

In therapy, I have asked many questions, mostly of myself. Over the years, I have accepted that not everything has an easy answer; nonetheless we ask, and we analyze. I have spent most of my adult life in therapy and many years taking various antidepressants and mood enhancers. I have also self-medicated and searched for numbness with alcohol.

I entered therapy always with one goal, to finish needing to come to therapy. It took years and maturity for me to accept that I was never going to be "cured." There won't be an "ah-ha" moment, where all the abuse that I endured will make sense. I needed to view therapy as a continuum of my existence. Constant exploration of self and constant questioning of the "truth." Now, I am simply focused on letting go of the shame, as I learn to love myself.

As various relatives aged and began to pass away, I felt an urgency to get some of my questions answered.

This time instead of asking Amma, I decided to call my youngest uncle, the only other living relative with a significant amount of knowledge of our family past. But first, I worked with my therapist to compose a set of questions that would help bring closure.

I messaged my uncle to give him a heads up of my call. I also reiterated that we needed privacy. With questions on a piece of paper, I called my uncle. After several rings, he picked up the phone.

I asked, "Is this a good time? I have some questions for you."

He replied, "Yes," with a confused tone.

I continued, "Mama, I just need to know. I am not looking to blame anyone. I just want to know, so I can be at peace."

He replied, "What?" as if the thought of me asking questions about my childhood had never crossed his mind.

"Please let me first read all my questions, nine of them. Then I will read one at a time for you to respond," I explained.

"Question number one, did all of you know that Amma was planning to go to Dinajpur and leave my sisters at Khala's house?"

My uncle quickly stopped me and responded, "Shama, that was a long time ago."

Before he could say anything further, I stopped him and said, "Please, let me finish going through my list of questions. Second, do you know why she took me with her?"

"Third, did Nani ever mention what took place in Dinajpur?"

"Fourth, did any of you know about the sleeping arrangement at Golam's place?"

"Five, when I returned to Dhaka, why was I kept separate from my sisters?"

"Six, did Khala not want me?"

"Seven, did you guys know about the physical abuse that Dhrobo Mama subjected on me?"

"Eight, when the decision was made to take all three of us to Dinajpur to either bring Amma back or leave us there, would you have left us there if Amma didn't come?"

And finally, "Have you ever talked with Amma about what took place in Dinajpur?"

I read the questions quickly before he could stop me again. I wanted to beg and say, please just tell me. But the moment I finished my list, I heard him sigh and take a deep breath.

"Shama, that was a long time ago. Why talk about the past?" he asked with a defensive tone. "Why talk about the dead?" he paused. "You are in America. You have a life and a family. Forget about this stuff."

"Mama, you are the only one left to give me some answers. I just want to know."

"I don't know anything," he replied.

Except I know some of the truth.

Mama was living at Nani's while I was there. Though he was in his late teens, he knew. And he too hit me on many occasions. Perhaps under normal circumstances, I would have listed him as one of my abusers, but comparatively, he was far less abusive than his brother or Golam.

I wanted to simply hang up and end my call when I realized that his loyalty to his sister was far greater than his loyalty to the truth. He chose to protect the memory of his mother and others despite my need for closure. Even though it was apparent that we would never discuss this topic again, I felt a sense of satisfaction knowing that he knew that I didn't forget. I wanted him, like Amma, to know that despite being a child, despite never mentioning Golam in front of them, I never forgot. I wanted them to know that I was no longer bound by shame or duty. I was no longer the keeper of the secret.

I said, "Well, that is all that I wanted to ask."

As I started to hang up, he responded "No matter what our parents do, Allah said that we must respect and honor them."

That was the last time I spoke with my uncle. Since that call, he has visited the States to see my mother. I heard of his visit but did not call him. He mentioned to my sister that he assumed that I was angry with him. Anger is a much easier emotion than hurt. I am not angry.

Boro Khala's son, Kazi, is ten years older than me. He is the only family member who ever listened to me, and to this day, he is the only one who has tried to find answers on my behalf. He was not in Dhaka when all these events took place. He was studying abroad.

The only recollection he has was his conversation with Abba in Memphis. My cousin was living in Memphis at the same time as Abba. Kazi told me that once he casually mentioned that Amma was in Dinajpur to Abba. Apparently, Abba got upset with him and said, "You don't know what you are talking about; your khala [Amma] is in Dhaka."

I had assumed that Amma's whereabouts were kept from Abba, and my cousin confirmed that for me. And on numerous occasions, Kazi mentioned that Dhrobo Mama had a mental illness, though I don't think that he was ever diagnosed. Consequently, he never received any treatments. Perhaps he was or perhaps that was the justification our family made for his volatile demeanor. Regardless, of being diagnosed or not, everyone knew that he was unstable, which left me to wonder why they left me to his care.

"His office is so far from your work; are you sure that he is worth the long drive?" my husband asked.

I was not a stranger to long roads. I had seen my childhood streets light up with a flash, then the loud sound of a bomb filled the air. I sat in the backseat of a car, sandwiched between my uncles, as we drove my father to the airport for his flight to America. I recall a plastic blanket draped over Amma and me, as we rode through dirty streets in Dinajpur on a rickshaw. Every pothole splattered muddy water on us, and we wiped it away without a second thought.

Those same rough roads were where my friends and I searched for daisies and escaped, as we gazed up to the sky, wanting to be noticed by Allah. We dropped down to our knees and dug our fingers into the dirt and filled our fists with Mother Earth.

I recalled the car rides where the flies flew in and out freely inspecting every content of our vehicle, as I sat in the back seat with Nani, ready to begin my new journey. Only a few years later, that same car drove us to the airport, and we climbed into an airplane for America. Sitting by a tiny window, I said goodbye to the rickshaws and masses of shoeless feet that filled the streets of Dhaka. I looked ahead, as our airplane charged the runaway with absolute force and took off into the clear blue sky.

Clinching a handwritten letter authored by my father, I rode the Memphis ISD school bus to my new school. I sat at the back of the Abrahams' van, as we drove to the hospital to say goodbye to Abba only to discover he was already gone. That same van carried my father's body to Munford for his burial. I looked out Akbor's car window as he and his father pointed to Abba's tombstone. It was the same car that I rode on my way to college, where I embarked yet on another new path.

In Austin, I drove myself from drugstore to drugstore, only to buy sleeping pills to end my life. I drove with my windows cracked, and the cold November wind blew inside. I drove without a care. Weeks later, I drove that same car to see my therapist Charles to discuss the hopeless roads that led me to my suicide attempt. It was there where I began to draft a new road map for the first time.

A few years later, I anxiously paced and waited, as a big stretch limo pulled up to my apartment complex; and from the third story window, I felt a sigh of relief. It was the sign that my husband-to-be was already at the courthouse waiting for me. I rode in that limo for the last time, as a single woman. Gazing out the window, I found it hard to relate to that girl in the rickshaw, yet there I was. There, I was sitting next to my husband, as he frantically drove to the hospital at 3:00 a.m. as my contractions grew closer.

I traveled many long roads, all void of my mother, but I was never alone. Imaginary friends and countless real friends had accompanied me on my journey. There were times when I just handed over the steering wheel and times when I fought all that stood in my path.

"THE LONG DRIVE back to my office after our sessions helps me to process what we discussed," I say to my husband about my therapy sessions with Owen.

But in reality, there were not fast, easy roads that could lead me to a better understanding of myself, especially my past.

I had followed Owen on Facebook for six months, reading his posts every day. I had read his entire website. I wanted to be sure that I was safe with him. I wanted a supportive environment, as I undertook my ride back through my childhood and began to give words to my pain. It is with that hope, I contacted Owen for my first appointment.

Sitting in heinous traffic, I told myself perhaps it was a bad idea. But common courtesy would not allow me to simply not show up, so I sent him an email saying, "On my way, stuck in traffic."

"This is a mistake," I said to myself by now twenty times. My GPS finally guided me to his building, and I reluctantly made my way to the second floor.

"I am late, horrible first impression. He probably thinks that I am a total loser. Good God don't call yourself a loser," I said to myself. "Shit, you need therapy." I had progressed to talking to myself in third person by the time I walked into his office.

Owen's waiting room was bright with several couches, shelves filled with books, magazines, and several different colors and sizes of pillows. I sat on the chair closest to the door, hoping that he wouldn't see me. From the corner of his door, I could see that he was on the computer when he heard me enter. He closed his laptop and came out with a smile. We shook hands, and I walked into his office. I scanned his office to look for a pillow, but there weren't any. I hesitantly sat down, and we began.

"He has an acrylic chair," I told my husband later that night.

"And?" Liam asked.

"It is transparent. You know, what does that mean? Does it mean that he is transparent, or does it mean that he wants his clients to be transparent?"

Before Liam could answer, I continued, "Or maybe he is saying that he 'sees' you."

Liam replied, "Or maybe he just likes acrylic furniture?"

"And he has a dog that bops its head. Why? And he doesn't have a pillow."

"Buy him a pillow, and don't look at the damn dog," my husband suggested.

"Anything else?" he asked.

"No," I replied.

I always walked into therapy with three objectives in mind, all leading me to the finish line. *I want answers; I want to be cured; and I want to be done with needing therapy*. I was tired of self-exploration. I was tired of looking at my past and evaluating the players, but more importantly— me. A few years ago, I realized that I was fighting the very vehicle that gave me the strength to drive. I had told myself the next time I found myself in therapy, I would not fight the process.

So, Owen and I began where I had left off or perhaps never traveled. I did not know if my long drive would lead me to the path that I had searched for all these years. But I embarked on this journey with an ever-changing road map.

I said to myself, *perhaps his acrylic chair is there to remind me that it is safe to be transparent and that I do not have to pretend to be accepted*. His office was where "just me" was enough even if it was for that hour. I could allow myself to be vulnerable. Owen would keep me safe. If I was driving, I was still alive.

My every other week appointments slowly became weekly. And Owen handed me a pillow from his waiting room before every session.

Looking out his window and stroking my faithful pillow, I asked, "Am I healed; am I cured?"

He knew that I was the only one who could answer, so we sat in silence for what felt like an eternity. We sat together, and we reflected on our journey. We reflected on the compassion, the trust, the courage. We reflected on the little girl whose resiliency afforded us this journey.

I broke the silence and said, "I have made a commitment to that little girl to live life celebrating every pocket of kindness that is showered upon me. I have committed myself to living, not just existing."

He smiled and handed me a daisy.

Epilogue

Writing this book did not come easily or quickly. It took years of therapy and self-reflection to find the courage to speak my truth. I did change the names of family members to honor their request for anonymity. However, I used my parents' actual names. I owe Abba the truth. Writing this book is my attempt to finally tell him my "secret."

I truly believe that we all do the best that we can with whatever tools that we have. Or at least I want to believe it. Otherwise, I will have to accept that my mother simply did not love me.

I do not know if she and/or others mentioned in this book suffered from mental illness. All I know is that I cannot begin to understand or forgive those who directly or indirectly took part in any form of child abuse. As society, we cannot justify the abusers' actions based on their own childhood experience. Although child abuse and trauma can have distressing, lifelong effects, it does not cause someone to abuse their own children later in life.

Since writing this book, both of my parents have passed away. Mother died in 2020, and due to COVID-19, I could not attend her funeral. Though, I can't with all honesty say that I would have attended under normal circumstances. My uncle Dhrobo and Nani died many years ago. Shashab and Golam, I can only assume are dead as well.

In 2016, my daughters and I visited Dhaka. It was their first visit to my birthplace. I relished in their joy as they tried sugarcane and rode a rickshaw for the first time. On the flight back to the States, they spoke of returning to Dhaka and of their fond memories.

I remain in touch with my cousins through social media and occasional phone calls. And they have visited me at my home in Texas. My cousin, Kazi, shared some childhood stories with me, as I tried to put the pieces of my childhood together. There may be some discrepancies with the timeline of my account. No living relatives from the time of my abuse helped with the collaboration of this book. But the details of my abuse in both Dinajpur and Azimpur are accurate to the best of my recollection. There are nights that I still wake up with Golam's smell consuming me.

Today, I live in Seattle with my partner, golden retriever, and our cat. I work for a nonprofit and remain an advocate for survivors of child abuse and exploitation. My daughters continue to be my absolute pride and joy. They have grown up to be two amazing, strong, young women. It is for them and for other survivors of abuse and exploitation that I continue to speak my truth.

Glossary

- **Abba:** Father
- **Amma**: Mother
- **Appa:** Sister
- **Khala*:** Aunt
- **Khalu**: Uncle
- **Mama*:** Uncle
- **Mami**: Aunt
- **Nana:** Grandfather
- **Nani**: Grandmother
- **Pir-Sufi:** Saint
- **Taka**: Bangladesh currency

*In Bangla, a woman's female sibling is referred to as Khala by her children and her husband as Khalu. A woman's male sibling is referred to as Mama by her children and his wife as Mami.

Acknowledgments

Writing a book is harder than I thought and more rewarding than I could have ever imagined. None of this would have been possible without my best friend, Amna Jaffer, who has been a nonjudgmental, loving constant in my life.

Writing a book about the story of your life is a surreal process. I'm forever indebted to Margo Dill, editor and publisher, and the members of the Writer's Garrett for their editorial help, keen insight, and ongoing support in bringing my stories to life. It is because of their efforts and encouragement that I have a legacy to pass on to my daughters.

To my daughters, Miriam and Mira, you are, and will always be, my greatest joy. You bring pure happiness to my life.

Finally, to all those who have been a part of my getting here: Jill C., Kelly H., and Lynda H., thank you for your friendship throughout the years. To Jim D., Jimmy O., and Christopher M., thank you for giving me a safe place to process. To Kazi & Tahiya S., thank you for your unconditional acceptance. And finally thank you to my partner, Curtis Ryan, for loving me.

About the Author

Shama Shams holds a master's degree in religion with an emphasis on Islam from Florida State University and a BA in political science from Agnes Scott College. In her spare time, Shama serves on several nonprofit boards.

She Called Me Throwaway is Shama's first book. Her second book, *From the Promise to the Pursuit - an American Dream*, is a heartfelt examination of the immigrant experience, a tribute to the indomitable spirit of those who embark on this journey, and an exploration of the evolving landscape of the American Dream is scheduled to be released in late 2024.

You can find out more about her and her writing on her website, www.writershama.com

More Editor-911 Books

Out of the Night that Covers Me

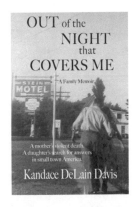

By Kandace DeLain Davis (Memoir, 2023)

A mother's violent death. A daughter's search for answers in small town America.

Left an orphan at six years old in 1976, Kandace DeLain Davis grew up in Crossville, Illinois, at her grandparents' kitschy roadside motor lodge. Seven years earlier, at the Anna State Hospital, Davis's mother, Mary Ellen Stein, had met her father at what was once known as The Illinois Southern Hospital for the Insane, after suffering from mental illness and addiction most of her adult life. When Mary Ellen was found dead in 1976 with a knife protruding from her chest, her family believed it must be suicide. Fast forward to 2015 when Davis discovered a tiny article from her local small town newspaper, dated not long after her mother's death, and Davis feared she may not have the full story. This newspaper clipping took her on a four-year journey, navigating through court documents and records of her mother's over one hundred hospitalizations, searching for the truth of her mother's death. Was this a case of die by suicide, or was she murdered?

I Hope I Find the Wind

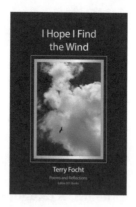

By Terry Focht (Poetry and Essays, 2022)

I Hope I Find the Wind is a lively collection of poetry and prose by poet Terry Focht. In these poems and reflections, Focht captures what matters most to all of us in life, but especially in his own, with themes of love and family, God and nature, historical events and cherished memories, overcoming adversity and hardships and hope and joy singing from the pages. Each poem makes you ponder life by offering a question, an observation or a masterfully woven image you will surely recognize from your own life: "How many footprints on winter's blanket?/ Where are they going those footprints of children on nature's quilt?"

He tackles tough subjects in this collection, too, such as his granddaughter's and wife's illnesses, children at the Mexico/U.S. border, a mother's exhausting work and social justice issues. However, he also has fun in this collection—you'll find yourself smiling at the poem, "Thinkin' About Stuff," when he writes, "The Secret of a Long Marriage/ Always say, "Yes, dear," / and you'll always be right./ The Worst Thing About Politics/ Politicians."

Not only has Focht created a unique event in each poem and essay, but also the book as a whole tells a story—the story of his life from a kid in the Rust Belt to a husband in love with his wife to a proud father and grandfather. The poems and reflections tell the story of a life, and readers will see themselves in these pages.

Even Before You Were Born

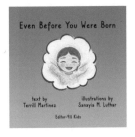

By Terrill Martinez (Gift book/Picture book, 2022)

A story for all children who are born first in the heart and imagination of their mothers.

Even Before You Were Born is the story of a mom who tells her daughter all the fun things she imagined they'd do together, even before she was born—from taking long walks together to loving her with her whole heart.

This beautifully written picture book by Terrill Martinez with vibrant and colorful illustrations by debut illustrator Sanaiya M. Luthar is the perfect book for parent and child to read together. It is sure to start discussions about what a parent imagines before their child is born—stories all children love to hear again and again.

As a love letter from a mom to her child, this book is also the perfect gift for a new mom (or soon-to-be new mom) who has her own hopes and dreams for her child.

Made in the USA
Columbia, SC
08 March 2024